JOUDIE KALLA

Palestine on a PLATE

Memories from my mother's kitchen

jacqui
small

Quarto is the authority on a wide range of topics.
Quarto educates, entertains and enriches the lives of
our readers – enthusiasts and lovers of hands-on living.
www.QuartoKnows.com

First published in 2016 by
Jacqui Small LLP
An imprint of Aurum Press
74–77 White Lion Street
London N1 9PF
Text copyright © 2016 by Joudie Kalla
Design, photography and layout copyright © Jacqui Small
    2016

Publisher: Jacqui Small
Senior Commissioning Editor: Fritha Saunders
Managing Editor: Emma Heyworth-Dunn
Project Manager and Editor: Abi Waters
Design and Art Direction: Manisha Patel
Photographer: Ria Osbourne
Prop Stylist: Lucy Harvey
Production: Maeve Healy

ISBN: 978 1 91025 474 5

A catalogue record for this book is available from the British
    Library.

2018 2017
10 9 8 7 6 5 4

Printed in China

When following the recipes, stick to one set of measurements
    (metric or imperial). Measurements used in the recipes are
    based on the following conversions:
25g = 1oz
1 tsp = 5ml
1 tbsp = 15ml
30ml = 1fl oz
240ml = 8fl oz = 1 cup (for both liquid and dry volume
    ingredients)

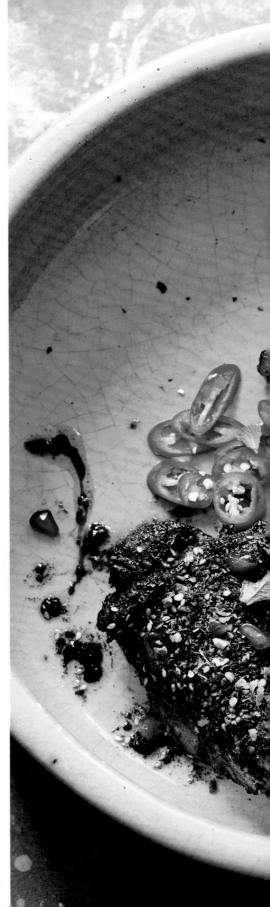

Contents

Introduction

My home is Palestine. Even though where I grew up wasn't geographically in Palestine, everything about our family life was Palestinian. Palestinian families have this innate yearning for community and it starts in the home. I lived with my siblings, aunties and parents and we were always together. Whether it was going on holiday, enjoying parties or simply having dinner, being together was what was important. The food we ate was always traditionally Palestinian, exactly what my parents had enjoyed when they were children. As we grew up, the dishes stayed the same, the food bonded us and helped to create a real sense of family – a Palestinian family.

My Journey

Regrettably, I was 21 before I was fluent in Arabic. My parents were very busy with five children, and even though they tried hard to give us lessons, we weren't very focussed. This all backfired one day when I was in Beirut on holiday with my family. I got lost and found myself alone. I could understand Arabic but couldn't speak the language, so I found it hard to communicate to anyone about where I lived and how to get there. Fortunately, I bumped into someone who knew my dad and who offered me a lift home, but this experience sparked something in me. I returned to London and began lessons every day with an amazing and very patient teacher and within a few months I had mastered the language.

After developing my linguistic skills in Arabic, everything changed for me. I became more interested in the food, culture and lifestyle and developed a curiosity about my Palestinian history and background. Every word in Arabic is so descriptive and poetic and has several meanings, which made me even more curious about this ancient, beautiful, historical world that I came from.

I also became aware of my westernized Arab friends. We were all far removed from our basic culture and background, despite having been so exposed to it during our adolescent years, but we all wanted to learn more about it. We were growing up, becoming independent, yet we also wanted to learn about our families' heritage and to have stories, memories and

recipes to pass on to our future families, which is inherent to keeping traditions and our culture alive. During this journey of discovery, it became clear that food was the main connection between us. It was the start of a journey that I am still on, and they are still on, too. Of course, we didn't all go on to become chefs, but we started going out to restaurants less often and dinner parties at home became more popular, where we began to share our stories and recipes. Everyone has their own versions of how to cook different dishes, which is great as we all add our own spin on things.

When I moved to Paris for my master's degree, I genuinely felt homesick as I had never lived away from home before. I stayed in an area where lots of Arabs lived, which only intensified my yearning for home. I saw all the bakeries and restaurants cooking things that we ate at home and that was it; my interest and need for knowledge about Palestinian cuisine began. I called my mother every day to ask her how to make the different dishes she had cooked for me when I was growing up. I learnt how to make *warak inab* (stuffed vine leaves), *makloubeh* (an upside-down rice dish with aubergines and lamb), *molokhia* (jute mallow leaves turned into a soup with chicken), and countless other dishes, and this is where my journey began as a chef. I left my degree course after six months and enrolled at Leith's School of Food and Wine in London. This experience opened my eyes to a world of discipline and order, commitment and hard work. My life changed from that moment on as I started on my professional food journey.

My restaurant, Baity Kitchen, was my outlet for all things Palestinian and delicious. I had Baity Kitchen in London for three wonderful years. Having to close the restaurant did not deter me though, as my clients were so supportive and encouraged me to start hosting monthly supper clubs in London (which has now grown into a successful catering business). My restaurant (and now my supper club) was like a hub for us all to sit and gather; not just Arabs, but people from all walks of life. Everyone who walked in felt at home, because the food reminded them of home.

Maintaining our Roots

Palestinian food is an identity. It is something that we hold very dear to our hearts as it is drenched in history from the generations that have passed. Palestinians are warm, homely, family-loving people; humble and devoted. Life is about living, giving and keeping Palestinian history very much alive. Celebrating and enjoying our cuisine and our roots is something we feel strongly about. This is how *Palestine on a Plate* began; to really share an understanding of dishes that have been cooked for hundreds, or even thousands of years. There are many debates about which dishes are truly Palestinian, but when looking through history books, photos and records you will find that the basis for many modern interpretations of dishes, like *makloubeh*, *mussakhan* or *m'sabaha* are all historically Palestinian and are a staple of the community.

The influence of other countries, and being located in the Levant, had a huge effect on the culture and cuisine in Palestine. Many influences came from Europe, Syria, Egypt, Turkey and Jordan. Dishes were changed and made to work with whatever ingredients were on offer and to hand. It is a land of ever-changing historical and cultural influences, but one that has always stuck to what it has known best over the years – simple, honest, flavourful food that is good for you. Each household has a family dish that they are extremely proud of and is part of their identity, and I hope in this book you will find something that will become a staple in your family home as well.

The History of Palestine

The land that became Palestine had a rich and colorful, albeit turbulent, experience throughout history. The region, or part of it, has come under the control of numerous different peoples, including: Paleo-Canaanites, Amorites, Ancient Egyptians, Israelites, Moabites, Ammonites, Tjeker, Philistines, Assyrians, Babylonians, Persians, Ancient Greeks, Romans, Byzantines, French Crusaders, Ayyubids, Mameluks, Ottoman Turks, the British, Jordanians in the West Bank and Egyptians in Gaza, and modern Israelis and Palestinians.

Islam became very prominent in this area of the Middle East after the battle of Yarmouk in 636 CE, and the Islamic Empire was firmly established in Palestine as Muslims conquered and ruled for over 1300 years. This time is referred to as the 'Golden age'. The land of Palestine has been populated by *Falasteniyeh* (Palestinians) since historical times and had a diverse religious outlook while predominantly being a Muslim country.

The first time there was a clear use of the name Palestine was in the 5th century BC in Greece, where it refers to the whole area encompassing Syria and Jordan. Herodotus wrote of a district of Syria called *Palaistine*. It appears again in 350 BCE from Aristotle where he wrote in *Meteorology*, 'Again if, as is fabled, there is a lake in Palestine, such that if you bind a man or beast and throw it in it floats and does not sink, this would bear out what we have said. They say that this lake is so bitter and salty that no fish live in it and that if you soak clothes in it and shake them it cleans them'. Aristotle was probably referring to the Dead Sea. Many writers such as Aristotle and Herodotus, and others like Pliny the Elder, Ovid and Tibullus, always used the name 'Palestine' to refer to this land and its inhabitants and this connection continues throughout history.

It was in this region, Palestine (the Holy Land), which was strategically placed at the centre of the Earth (according to medieval times) and home to the three biggest religions (Islam, Christianity and Judaism), that some of the earliest habitation, culture and agricultural activity took place. Through the different styles of cooking, Palestinians have successfully created a delicious combination of foods, a cuisine, that is fast becoming a staple in homes all around the world.

Palestine is a country of many different faces, where a wealth of different religions, culture and history can be found in the different areas of the country. If you visit places such as Al-Quds (Jerusalem) you will find yourself in a completely different world compared to other areas in Palestine – it is a melting pot of life, religion, culture and cuisine.

As a nation, Palestinians are determined and eager to preserve our cuisine and our heritage. The basic ingredients, recipes and cooking methods are very similar across the Middle East, which means you will often find many different versions of a similar dish. Although the history of Palestine is complex and fascinating, in this book I wish to celebrate the beauty of our food, and the food traditions that we are trying to keep alive. There is a chance that you have already eaten Palestinian food without realising it. In this book I want to champion our cuisine, recapture it and let the spotlight fall on our wonderful ways and hundreds of years of traditions and recipes. After all, what is more fundamental to a people's history and culture than their food?

Middle Eastern Flavours

Middle Eastern food is shrouded in mystery with ingredients and names of dishes that can be difficult to pronounce, but the beauty is that it's actually very simple and delicious. From the colourful sugar-free breakfasts like *mana'eesh*, labneh, *fattet hummus* and *ful mudammas*, to humble yet glorious lunches and dinners full of garlic, spices, chillies and herbs. Middle Eastern food should not be daunting. It should be exciting and wonderful, a treat to make and have every day if you can. It is full of vibrant colours, textures and flavours and is easy on the

palate. The tradition is to have many dishes on the table at a time – a celebration at every meal. To offer food in abundance is how I have been taught to eat and enjoy food by my family.

Palestinians eat a combination of salads, vegetables, meat and fish at every meal. This means guests or family members always have a choice. Salads and vegetables are an extremely important part of the dinner table (about 60 percent of our cuisine is made up of vegetarian dishes). A tomato salad is never just a simple plate of tomatoes on a Palestinian table – it will be drizzled with olive oil, sprinkled with sumac, ripped mint leaves, a bit of za'atar and salt flakes. There is always something extra added.

The aromas of cinnamon, nutmeg, spices and herbs were always wafting through our house. Even after leaving Palestine, my grandmothers brought Palestine with them and instilled this into my parents. It lives with us because of everything we do. Our family lives, our food culture, our history and our devotion to our country. We are Palestinian before we are anything else. From our orange blossom sugar syrups to rose water puddings, our home was always sweet-smelling and filled with love.

Food is everything for Arabs. When we are eating breakfast we are talking about lunch, and when we are eating lunch we are talking about dinner, and then thinking about what we will eat to break our fast in the morning. This is a universal discussion amongst Arabs at the dinner table or in the kitchen. It is something that keeps our culture and heritage alive.

The Food of Palestine

In the last few years there has been a surge in restaurants offering a new kind of Middle Eastern cuisine, which always includes a hint of Palestine. The diverse and colourful history of the Middle East has created a cuisine that is healthy, vibrant and delicious. Each country within the region has its own version of food and cooking style depending

on what ingredients were available. Certain basic recipes are staples across the Middle East but with different ingredients added from region to region, resulting in many variations of the same dish. An example of this is *fasoulia bil lahme*, where the Palestinian version uses green beans, the Lebanese version uses butter beans and the Egyptian version uses runner beans.

The recipes in this book use the methods and ingredients that I have learned from my mother and grandmothers and are truly Palestinian at heart (even though there might be similar versions from other regions in the Middle East). Before the Nakba (Palestinian exodus) in 1948 led them to Syria, my grandmothers had never travelled and only knew the Palestinian way of preparing these dishes.

Palestine, due to its geographical location, was influenced by its neighbours. From the North in Safad (where my father is from) and Galilee to the South East in Al-Lydd (where my mother is from) and down to Jerusalem and Gaza, the food differs but is united at the same time, through love and history. What I have gathered from speaking to my relatives back home and to my family here, is summed up by a much-used sentence – 'What was feasible and what we could afford' – in other words, make something wonderful from whatever ingredients were to hand. From this came some delicious dishes that we grew up with here in London, and that never lacked in nutrition, flavour, diversity or colour.

Palestinian food is found in the home. That is where it all begins. Of course you can find stalls with *za'atar mana'eesh* (za'atar flat breads) and *knafeh* (sweet cheese pastries) or places where they simply sell falafel, but the real cooking is done at home where it is seeped in history. I remember my mother cooking about five dishes a night for us all. They would include some sort of salad or starter like *salatet fattoush* (traditional mixed salad with za'atar and crunchy toasted pita) or *salatet arnabeet ma' tahineh* (oven-baked cauliflower with tahini sauce), with two or three main courses, such as *maftoul* (hand-rolled semolina balls cooked with caraway and chicken), *malfouf* (stuffed cabbage rolls with caraway and garlic) and *sayyadiyeh* (cumin and lemon marinated white fish served on cumin onion rice with caramelized onions and tahini dressing). My mother made it seem so easy to recreate, as she made the dishes with great flair and love.

I have changed some of my mother's recipes as I was writing this book, to make them less fatty, less fussy and less time consuming; and she has now adopted these versions of the old recipes, too. After all, who has all day to spend cooking? The recipes in this book will take traditional Palestinian cooking to a new dimension, changing some of the more traditional methods, and most importantly reducing the amount of time it takes to prepare and cook these dishes. From what I remember, the meals we ate at home would take my mother hours, if not days, to prepare. With today's rushed lifestyle, I am trying to reconnect and be true to the past, while being mindful of everyone's modern, busy lives.

Cooking with Love

Living in a big family meant that, growing up, our lives were always filled with people. I remember our friends used to come over and would end up staying for dinner even though they hadn't intended to stay that long. They would beg their mothers to let them stay and eat my mum's food as it was so delicious and so very different to what they ate at home.

When our grandmothers came to stay from Palestine, the house became a mess, and I mean this in a good way. My mother and her sisters would sit with my grandmothers Najla and Huda, discussing the most important thing, dinner! They would tell stories of who liked to eat what, how my father refused to eat this or that, and that since he met my mother he had changed his eating habits – all while cooking up a feast for us. It was so important to them to make sure their loved ones liked their food and that they were able to feed their children a variety of things. I was always in the kitchen with my mother and aunties and this is where I found peace and creativity. I loved the chats, the stories, the little disagreements about how much of this and how much of that should go into a dish, and most of all the sense of togetherness that this created. I am totally indebted to my mother, my aunties and my grandmothers for their love and passion for food and that it managed to seep into my life. It grounded me and has had a huge influence on me.

I have always admired how much effort and work it took my relatives to make things in the kitchen, but the joy at the end result was all that mattered. I then experienced this first hand as a chef working in professional kitchens; seeing my plates come back empty and having comments from the staff that a customer loved this or loved that – it really is why I cook. If you cook from a place a love, you will receive the best compliment in the form of an empty dish at the end of a meal.

Palestine is such a huge part of who I am and how I cook. Everything to me has a story, a feeling, a thought and a memory, and this is how I cook on a daily basis. I am governed by how I feel and what mood I am in. The same dish can be created from totally differing feelings of nostalgia, happiness, homesickness and so many other emotions, but the

reality is, the food always makes me feel at peace when I am eating. And I always make more than I need, as leftovers are the best. We serve big portions in my house and I also did in my restaurant. That's why people came back. A hearty dish is a dish that is filled with love, as my mother says.

I believe food should be visually beautiful, since you eat with your eyes first – and that is exactly what Palestinian food is. The next most important thing is the flavour, which should outshine the appearance, and I think this is where Palestinian food really comes into its own.

Palestine on a Plate is my tribute to my family, my mother, my home. These are old recipes that were created with love in a very different time to those we live in today. The images, stories and culture of Palestine are reflected in the food in this book. It is for everyone who loves food, understands the history of food and how it all relates to Palestine. It is for those who are lucky enough to have eaten Palestinian food and for those who are about to find out about it in this book. I want to pay homage to my family who were born there before our borders were changed and shifted; to the Palestine that my family knew and remembers.

'Sometimes a homeland becomes a tale. We love the story because it is about our homeland and we love our homeland even more because of the story.'

Refaat Alareer, *Gaza Writes Back*

My World of Ingredients

Palestinian food is filled with spices and herbs from all over the world. Palestine is situated between the Mediterranean sea and the Jordan river, and this strategic point makes it a successful trade route between Europe, Asia and Africa; it is known as the western end of the Fertile Crescent where trade flourished. There were several trade routes running through Palestine, but the two most important ones were 'the way of the sea' and 'the ridge route'. These provided opportunities to explore new and wonderful ingredients but also left Palestine vulnerable to conquerors, with invasions happening many times. The ridge route went through the valleys between Jordan and the foothills of the Mediterranean sea, whereas the sea route allowed traders from as far afield as Asia to deliver goods to the ports of Gaza. Spices and herbs were frequently transported through Palestine on the trade routes, which meant they soon became very much a part of Palestinian cuisine and of traditional Palestinian dishes, such as *Sayyadiyeh* (Cumin and Lemon Cod Served on Cumin Rice with Caramelized Onions and Tahini Tarator Sauce, see page 169) and *Makloubeh* ('Upside Down' Spiced Rice with Lamb and Aubergines, see page 122).

My world of ingredients is full of herbs and spices. My pantry is always well stocked – I buy ingredients in bulk so that I never run out. From an early age, I learnt this from my mother, who learnt from her mother, and I shall continue this way with my family.

Spices & Herbs

Baharat Spice Mix

This spice blend is made from a range of spices and is used as a marinade for meats, in stews and sometimes on fish, but very sparingly as it can be quite overwhelming. It is delicious and packed full of flavour. Use the following recipe if you want to prepare your own spice blend at home:

1 small dried chilli
1 teaspoon black peppercorns
3 teaspoons cumin seeds
1 teaspoon ground cinnamon
1 cardamom pod
1 teaspoon paprika
2 teaspoons coriander seeds
1 teaspoon ground nutmeg
1 teaspoon *loomi* (dried limes), blitzed to a powder
1 teaspoon sea salt

Use a spice grinder to blitz all of the above together to create a smooth powder. Taste, to ensure you are happy with the flavour and adjust if needed. This can be stored in an airtight container for several months.

Caraway

Caraway is thought to be of Middle Eastern origin and is native to Asia, Europe and North Africa. The flavour is complicated to describe – it is almost aniseed-like but not quite as strong and has the hint of fennel and something else I can't quite put my finger on. I use it in *Malfouf* (Garlic and Caraway Stuffed Cabbage Leaves, see page 143), as it brings out the flavours of everything in the dish so perfectly. We also make a tea by simply infusing caraway seeds in boiling water.

Cardamom

Cardamom arrived in Palestine from countries such as India, Bangladesh, Indonesia and Nepal. This spice, which in Arabic is called *hail*, is used in our traditional Arabic coffee to give it a distinct flavour. We usually use the green cardamom pods, often to flavour rice dishes and meat stews. It is also used in teas to soothe pains and truly adds a flavour of the Middle East when used in cakes and desserts.

Cumin

Cumin dates back as far as the second millennium BC and has been transported through trade from India to Syria, Egypt and, most notably, Iran, as

1 Loomi (Dried lime)
2 Za'atar
3 Cardamom pods
4 Sumac
5 Chilli flakes
6 Dried rose buds
7 Maftoul
8 Freekeh
9 Labneh

well as to Palestine. It is mentioned in the bible in the New and Old Testament and has been used in cooking for its flavour and for medicinal purposes too. It was introduced to America by the Spanish and Portuguese colonists who had travelled through the Mediterranean and Asia. The most common cumin seeds are the black and green ones. The green seeds are most commonly used in Palestinian cooking, as they are slightly younger and more aromatic. Cumin is used in teas to soothe stomach aches and also in one of our national dishes in Palestine, *Sayyadiyeh* (Cumin and Lemon Cod Served on Cumin Rice with Caramelized Onions and Tahini Tarator Sauce, see page 169). It aromatizes and gives a smoky flavour to dishes.

Dried Chilli Flakes

These are crushed, not ground and made from cayenne chillies so they vary in heat. They are used in many Palestinian dishes to add a kick of chilli heat.

Dukkah

Dukkah is an earthy Middle Eastern mix blended from roasted, stone-ground wheat and toasted sesame seeds. Nuts are sometimes added, but it depends on where you are from in the Middle East and a matter of taste. I like mine with hazelnuts added, for example, but in Syria they often add crushed pistachios. I use dukkah on egg dishes and also as a dip for warm toasted pita bread by mixing it with Palestinian olive oil. Use the following recipe if you want to prepare your own spice blend at home:

50g (1¾oz) hazelnuts, skinned

3 tablespoons coriander seeds

2 teaspoons cumin seeds

1 teaspoon fennel seeds

2 tablespoons sesame seeds

1 teaspoon paprika

1 teaspoon dried marjoram

1 teaspoon sea salt

Toast the nuts in an oven preheated to 180°C fan (200°C/400°F/Gas 6) for about 15–20 minutes until slightly toasted in colour. Toast the coriander, cumin and fennel seeds together in a hot dry frying pan for about 30–40 seconds. Remove the pan from the heat and set the seeds aside. Add the sesame seeds to the hot pan and toast for about 1 minute until slightly toasted. Grind the toasted coriander, cumin and fennel seeds to a powder, then place them in a bowl. Add the sesame seeds, paprika and marjoram. Chop the nuts into small pieces and add them with the salt and stir. This can then be stored in an airtight container for several months.

Paprika

Paprika is made from the dried chilli peppers from the capsicum family. It is used as a flavour and also to add colour to dishes. The popularity of paprika has stretched from Iberia to Africa and through to Asia on the trade routes and it is now a widely used ingredient in cooking. I love this spice as it's smoky and also occasionally hot. I use this in my *Hindbeh* (dandelion leaves) recipe on page 84 to add flavour and colour.

Ras el Hanout

This beautiful spice blend originated in North Africa. It is used in tagines and as a base for many North African dishes. I rub this on meat and fish to create an earthy, fragrant flavour. I also like to sprinkle it on root vegetables. It is a deliciously complex and aromatic blend of cumin seeds, ginger, turmeric, coriander seeds, allspice, nutmeg and chillies. You can use the following recipe to make your own version at home:

2 dried red chillies

2 teaspoons cumin seeds

1 teaspoon ground ginger

2 teaspoons coriander seeds

1 teaspoon ground turmeric

2 teaspoons ground allspice

½ teaspoon ground nutmeg

1 teaspoon sea salt

Mix the ingredients in a spice grinder to a smooth powder. Transfer to a jar to keep for several months.

Sumac

Sumac is a spice that comes from the sumac tree. It goes well with pretty much everything, from salads to meat and fish, pastries and as a garnish. The sumac tree can grow to almost 10 metres tall and has clusters of sumac buds, which are dried and used to create this crimson powder, which has a tangy, citrusy taste. It is considered to be a powerful antioxidant and has been used for medicinal purposes since the 13th century.

Za'atar

This is probably the most famous ingredient used in Palestinian cooking. It is a herb and spice mix that can be used on its own for dipping, rubbing on meats and fish and sprinkling on salads, and is sold on street corners in Palestine in flat breads called *Mana'eesh Za'atar* (Fluffy Za'atar Sesame Breakfast Bread, see page 43). There are many varieties, but to try an authentic version it must be Palestinian as the native thyme and spices offer a superior flavour. There is a belief that za'atar makes the mind alert and body strong, and children have long been encouraged to eat this in a sandwich for breakfast to set them up for the day. You can easily make this blend yourself at home by following the recipe below:

4 tablespoons dried thyme

1 tablespoon dried marjoram

3 tablespoons toasted sesame seeds

1½ teaspoons sumac

1 teaspoon sea salt

Blitz the thyme and marjoram together in a food processor or blender until just mixed, but not to a pure powder. Add the sesame seeds, sumac and salt and mix. This is when you can try different measurements of the different ingredients in order to work out your personal preference. I tend to prefer mine with a more nutty flavour so I usually add more sesame seeds. But feel free to experiment. This can be stored in an airtight container for several months.

Grains & Pulses

Burghul (Cracked Wheat)

Burghul was very popular in all regions of the Ottoman Empire, which is why there are several names for it. Burghul is used in much of Northern Palestine due to its mountainous regions and is used as a bulking component to recipes. It is a whole grain that is high in fibre and is wonderfully nutty in flavour. We have coarse burghul and fine burghul, which are used very differently. I have used fine burghul to make *Kubbeh Bil Sanniyeh* (Burghul and Spiced Minced Lamb Pie, see page 78) and coarse burghul to make *Burghul Wa Kousa* (Burghul with Courgettes and Spicy Tomato Sauce, see page 108). It is very common in Middle Eastern cuisine and in northern India, where it is called *dalia*.

Freekeh

This is one of the greatest grains we have in Palestine. It is a young toasted green wheat that is harvested in the sun and then set on fire to create a charred effect on the outside, while protecting the seeds. It then goes back in the sun to intensify the flavour. This process is called *farik*, which literally means rubbed, and gives freekeh its name. Freekeh has at least four times more fibre than other grains, which makes it a superfood in my book. It can also help to manage diabetes as it is a good source of slow-burning energy. The whole of the Middle East uses this versatile and delicious grain, but in Palestine we use it most commonly in many savoury dishes and desserts, such as *Shorabet Freekeh* (Freekeh Soup, see page 54), *Fil Fil Mahshi Bil Freekeh* (Freekeh-stuffed Peppers, see page 57) and *Salatet Djaj Wa Freekeh* (Freekeh Salad with Marinated Chicken and Pomegranate Dressing, see page 58). It is used in countless dishes to create an earthy, smoky flavour.

Maftoul (Palestinian Pearl Cous cous)

Maftoul are hand-rolled balls of semolina that are used to make hearty dishes that are low in cost and very filling. They have traditionally been made by hand by housewives in Palestine and are a popular ingredient. The original name for this ingredient is *keksku* from the Berber, which means 'well rolled'. It then became known as *maftoul* in Arabic, which comes from the verb 'fa-ta-la', which means 'to roll or twist'. *Maftoul* can be traced back to North Africa

10 Light fine burghul
11 Dark coarse burghul
12 Light coarse burghul
13 Brown lentils
14 Ground caraway
15 Ras el hanout
16 Paprika
17 Cumin seeds
18 Fennel seeds

19 Egyptian rice
20 Dried brown broad beans
21 Palestinian olive oil
22 Vermicelli nest
23 Pomegranate molasses
24 Blanched almonds
25 Tahini
26 Dukkah
27 Pistachios
28 Raw pine nuts

from as early as the 13th century and is known as a national dish in that region. Its popularity spread like wildfire across the Middle East and Europe, changing size and cooking method depending on who was making it – in North Africa they are generally a little smaller than in Palestine for example, and in Lebanon they are relatively large, like chickpeas. *Maftoul* is a very popular dish in Palestine made with chicken, chickpeas, *maftoul*, caraway seeds and caramelized onions (see page 71).

Chickpeas & Brown Broad Beans

When I cook with chickpeas and beans I often use the tinned variety for ease and to save time. But on certain occasions I use dried chickpeas and brown broad beans as the tinned varieties will not produce the right effect (they are too soggy and waterlogged). In a recipe such as Falafels (see page 72), for example, you will need to use dried chickpeas that are soaked overnight and then gently boiled the next day for about 20–30 minutes. Tinned chickpeas hold too much water for a recipe like this and you would find the resulting falafels would fall apart when you came to moulding and frying them. Dried chickpeas are simple and easy to cook with; it's just a matter of timing and planning your meal. The same applies for broad beans. *Ful mudammas* (dark brown broad beans) are pre-Ottoman and pre-Islamic and thought to be as old as the Pharaohs. They are cooked and dressed with garlic, chillies and herbs and are truly a wonderful ingredient that is used all over the Middle East. You can find the dark brown beans dried or tinned in Middle Eastern stores and they are often called *ful mudammas* on the tin as that is what they are most commonly used for.

Sha'riyeh (Vermicelli Nests)

This type of pasta is commonly cooked with rice in Palestine. You will sometimes find white basmati rice cooked by itself but when it is cooked with vermicelli it almost makes a dish on its own. The *sha'riyeh* is toasted and then boiled with the rice, creating a nutty backdrop and adding another dimension to dishes, such as in *Fasoulia Bil Lahme* (String Beans with Lamb Cooked in a Garlicky Tomato Sauce, see page

145) and *Sabanekh Wa Ruz Bil Sha'riyeh* (Spinach Stew with Vermicelli Rice, see page 93). You can also use them in desserts, as I have done in this book.

Fruits, Nuts & Seeds

Dibs Rumman (Pomegranate Molasses)

Dibs Rumman is a syrup made from pomegranate juice that has been reduced to a thick, dark liquid. It is sticky and sour and goes with everything – stews, pastas, meat, salads – this is one ingredient I'd take with me to a dessert island! I have bottles and bottles of it in my cupboards at home.

Loomi (Dried Lime)

Dried limes are known as black limes and are dehydrated in the sun. They originated in the Persian Gulf and are used in lots of stews in the Middle East, especially a wonderful dish originating from Kuwait called *Mashbous* (Loomi and Spiced Chicken Rice Platter, see page 164). It is used to add sourness to dishes and has a wonderfully aromatic flavour. You can use them whole or grind them to a powder.

Almonds

Almonds are native to the Middle East, but have been sold on the trade routes as far as India, Pakistan and Iran. Their popularity spread quickly to North Africa and to Europe. Almonds are always used blanched and with their skins removed in Palestinian cooking and are used in both savoury and sweet dishes.

Pine Nuts

Middle Eastern pine nuts are slender and long and are probably the best you can get. However, if you can't find any in Middle Eastern shops, by all means use what you find in the supermarket. Pine nuts are often scattered over the top of dishes as a garnish, but in reality the dish would not be the same without them. They are beautifully subtle in flavour but carry their weight in any dish they are in. I usually toast them in butter in a hot frying pan until they just turn golden brown as this releases their flavour.

Pistachios

Pistachio trees are one of the oldest flowering trees, dating back to even earlier than 5000 BC. The trees are native to the Middle East, Iran and Asia, and the nuts have been imported on trade routes to countries like Italy and other parts of Europe. They are most commonly used in desserts and not in our main savoury meals as you will find in Persian cuisine. They are wonderful crushed over sweet syrupy desserts like *Ruz Bil Haleeb* (Creamy Orange Blossom Rice Pudding with Dried Roses, see page 209).

Tahini

This has to be THE ingredient that I associate most with the Middle East. It is a gorgeous creamy, nutty toasted sesame paste that is used in so many of our dishes it seems that most things wouldn't work without it. It is great mixed with tomatoes, parsley and lemon juice and drizzled over salads, or used as a dip for bread. Creamy tahini appears in several dishes in this book as it is my favourite accompaniment. Use it on fish, meat and salads and it works perfectly well; so diverse and flavourful. I even use it in brownies (see page 216). To make delicious tahini at home, follow this recipe:

300g (10½oz) sesame seeds
2 tablespoons olive oil

Toast the seeds in a hot dry frying pan until golden brown. Put them in a food processor or blender and blitz until the oils are released and it becomes a thick paste. Add the oil to loosen, but only do this once you have a paste otherwise it will not become smooth. Keep blitzing until you reach a consistency you are happy with, adding more oil if needed. Transfer to a jar and keep refrigerated for 2–4 weeks.

Other Flavourings

Edible Dried Rose Buds

Roses have been used in cooking, teas and syrups for centuries and are a staple of Palestinian cooking. They most probably originated in countries such as India and Iran, and then were sold on the trade routes and became popular in Palestine. These decorative and lightly perfumed rose buds are sprinkled over desserts and steeped in teas to add a floral taste to Palestinian food. They are also very beautiful and really make a dish stand out. Be sure to always buy edible dried buds for use in cooking.

Labneh (Strained Yogurt)

Labneh is a yogurt that has been strained to remove its whey, becoming thick and creamy and slightly tart. We eat labneh with za'atar and olive oil and dipped with bread (see page 39). It is also served with tomatoes and sumac or dried mint for breakfast.

Ma'zaher (Orange Blossom Water)

Orange blossom water is distilled water infused with fresh orange blossoms and is used to aromatize many of our desserts and sugar syrups. *Ma'zaher* is very prevalent in North African cuisine, especially tagines, and is being used increasingly in British, American and Spanish cooking. *Ma'zaher* is used in most of the desserts in this book in some form or another. It is not used in savoury cooking as it is in Persia, but it is added to coffees and used in desserts in Palestine and is synonymous with the Middle East.

Palestinian Olive Oil

Palestinian olive trees are rain fed and hand picked. The olives are also pressed on the day of harvest, creating a vibrant green peppery oil that is organic by nature. Palestinian olive oil tends to be made by people who see their trees both as old friends and as a lifeline for their families for generations to come. Be sure to buy from Zaytoun CIC (see page 236), who produce, for me, the best olive oil I have tried.

Rose Water

This perfumed liquid is made by mixing together water and rose petals, leaving them to infuse before heating them for about 1–1½ hours to intensify the flavour. You are then left with a mix of rose oil and rose water, which will separate naturally. It is a very popular flavour enhancer in Palestinian desserts and in some savoury dishes. It can also be used in cosmetics and for medicinal purposes too.

Good Morning Starters

My siblings and I always knew our breakfast was different to the breakfasts our friends ate at home. Our mother would also give us the more popular breakfasts of cornflakes with milk or scrambled eggs on toast, but the truth is, they never tasted as good as my parents' breakfasts. Theirs seemed so decadent and almost gluttinous, with olive oil dripping off their fingers, dipping breads into za'atar and labneh, coating each bite with deliciousness. I felt cheated, so began to try all these exciting dishes for myself. The savoury breakfast for me is a dream. I will almost never have pastries or sweet things for breakfast, as I love that savoury taste to linger in my mouth. This is a selection of my favourite dishes to start the day – full of colours, flavours and memories of back home. Like a ray of sunshine on a plate.

Ijeh

Fluffy Egg Fritters with Tomato Salsa

Ijeh, a herby egg fritter, is one of those dishes that I think came about purely by accident when someone had leftovers and just threw everything in the pan with some eggs and, hey presto, you have a wonderful flavour-packed breakfast with a kick. This colourful dish has a great balance of sharp and tangy against the smoothness of the eggs. My mother would cook this whenever we were moaning about how hungry we were, as it is so quick to whip up and kept everyone satisfied until lunchtime. This egg fritter is sublime with its chilli tomato topping that hits just the right spot every time. Never disappointing.

Serves 4

1 small onion, finely chopped

1 green chilli, chopped

8 eggs, beaten

1–2 garlic cloves, finely
   chopped or grated
   (I use 2 for an added kick)

1½ tablespoons plain flour

¼ teaspoon baking powder

1 tablespoon dried mint

1 tomato, deseeded and
   cubed

a bunch of fresh flat-leaf
   parsley, chopped

a small bunch of fresh chives,
   chopped

a few leaves of fresh mint,
   chopped

sea salt and black pepper

vegetable or sunflower oil,
   for frying

For the salsa:

2 large tomatoes, finely
   chopped

juice of 2 lemons

200ml (7fl oz) olive oil

1 garlic clove, grated

a sprinkle of dried mint

a small bunch of fresh
   flat-leaf parsley, chopped

To make the salsa, mix all the ingredients together with a pinch of salt and set aside until needed.

Mix all the *ijeh* ingredients, except the oil, together in a bowl to make a batter.

Heat a teaspoon of oil in a frying pan over a high heat until it's very hot. Drop ladlefuls of the batter into the hot pan in batches (adding more oil for each fritter) and cook for about 2 minutes until they are lightly browned. Turn the fritters over to cook the other side for another 2 minutes, then lay them on a plate and keep warm while you continue cooking – or serve to whoever is waiting for them so they can eat as you cook.

Serve the fritters with the salsa.

Tip: You should use the batter straightaway as it contains baking powder – the fritters will not get the desired fluffy effect if the batter is kept standing for long.

Bayd Ma' Sujuk

Spicy Lamb Sausage with Scrambled Eggs

Sujuk is a deliciously spiced, tangy sausage used in the Middle East, which my mother loved to add to our eggs to make them a little more interesting. These little sausages (they are smaller than your little finger) are generally sold in Middle Eastern stores, but if you can't find them you can use the meat mixture from the *Fatayer* recipe on page 146 as a good substitute.

Serves 2

2 tablespoons olive oil

12 *sujuk* (spicy sausage), cut into halves, or more if you prefer

6 eggs

a pinch of sea salt

Heat the oil in a pan over a medium heat. Add the *sujuk* and cook for about 3–4 minutes, releasing the colour and flavour.

Once the *sujuk* has cooked, crack and scramble the eggs in the same pan and add the salt. I like my eggs slightly runny so I only cook them for 1–2 minutes over a medium heat.

Serve with some *Khubez* (pita bread, see page 48) and enjoy the flavour of the Middle East.

Soft Boiled Eggs with Za'atar Soldiers

Everyone likes their eggs cooked in different ways. I like mine runny and gooey. Instead of just using plain toast to dip in to the runny yolks, I like to make the toast the star of the meal by coating pita bread in deliciously herby za'atar.

Serves 4

1 *Khubez* (pita bread, see page 48), cut into strips

2 tablespoons olive oil

2 tablespoons za'atar (see page 17), or more if you prefer

4 eggs

sea salt

Preheat the oven to 180°C fan (200°C/400°F/Gas 6). Line a baking tray with baking parchment.

Coat the pita strips with olive oil. Put the za'atar in a bowl, dip half of each pita strip into the za'atar and press to make the herby mix stick. Place the pita strips on the lined baking tray and bake for 5–6 minutes until crisp.

Meanwhile, cook the eggs in a saucepan of boiling water for 6 minutes (or cook to your liking).

Remove the tops of the eggs and season them with salt. Serve with the za'atar soldiers.

Bayd Wa Lahmeh Ma' Salatat Jarjir
Scrambled Eggs & Minced Lamb with Rocket & Purslane Salad

When my siblings and I were younger, this dish would appear on the dining table frequently. It is a delicious combination of creamy, spiced minced lamb scrambled into eggs and served with a tangy salad. Growing up, when we returned home late after a night out, we would often stay up even later, chatting with friends about what had happened that night, and soon enough we would realize it was now the early hours of the morning, and our stomachs would rule the conversation. As this is so easy to put together, I would whip it up and we would have a little mini breakfast before going to bed.

Serves 4

4 tablespoons sunflower oil

400g (14oz) lamb mince

a bunch of purslane

a bunch of rocket

1 small red onion, cut in half and sliced

2 tablespoons white wine vinegar

4 tablespoons olive oil

10 eggs, beaten

a small bunch of fresh flat-leaf parsley

sea salt and black pepper

Heat a frying pan and add the sunflower oil. Add the lamb mince and cook until browned. Add some salt and pepper to taste.

Meanwhile, put the purslane, rocket and onions in a salad bowl and mix in the vinegar, olive oil and some salt, then set aside.

Once the lamb has cooked, add the eggs and parsley and scramble them quickly through the mixture – it should cook within 3–4 minutes.

Serve the eggs and lamb with the salad on the side.

Kibdet Il Djaj
Spicy Chicken Livers with Coriander & Lemon

Liver is one of those foods that you either love or hate – I LOVE it. Be it duck liver, goose liver, chicken liver or calves liver, I love them all. They all have different textures, flavours and strengths, but the easiest to use is chicken liver. It is quick to cook and so versatile – it can be made into a paté or simply fried quickly and served as it is. My mum makes this liver dish often and I now make it all the time when I am hungry and need a quick fix of food with minimum fuss. One packet of store-bought chicken livers can be enough to feed two people, but I always make more than I need as it is so moreish – I can guarantee you'll want second helpings. I also often add pomegranate seeds and extra fresh coriander before serving for an extra zing.

Serves 2

150ml (5fl oz) olive oil

1 large onion, cut in half and sliced

3 garlic cloves, sliced

400g (14oz) organic chicken livers

a handful of plain flour, seasoned with sea salt and pepper

juice of 1–2 lemons

1 green jalapeño, chopped

a bunch of fresh coriander

sea salt

Heat the oil in a frying pan, add the onion and garlic and cook over a gentle heat for about 10 minutes until the onions have caramelized.

Meanwhile, clean away any veins or bloody extracts from the chicken livers, then rinse them well with water. Coat the livers with the seasoned flour.

Use a slotted spoon to remove the onions from the pan and set aside. Increase the heat to high. Add the livers to the pan, let them sear without moving them in the pan, for 3–4 minutes until they have browned on one side. Turn them over and brown the other sides (depending on how you like your livers cooked).

Squeeze in some of the lemon juice and cook through for a few minutes. Take care not to overcook them, or they will be tough and chewy.

Add the jalapeño and stir through, then add half the coriander and mix well. You can taste a little to see if you need more of something – I usually end up using the juice of 2 lemons and a sprinkle of salt as I love sour-tasting food, and a lot of chilli.

After about 6–8 minutes the livers should be caramelized on the outside and pink on the inside. Take the pan off the heat, mix the onions back into the pan, and add the remaining coriander and stir through. You can serve with rice, freekeh or just plain with toasted pita bread.

Tip: Liver is full of vitamin A and cod liver oil, which are both great for your body. They help with your bones, eyesight and growth, so it is highly recommended that you eat liver at least once a month. I much prefer to eat fresh chicken livers than to take a vitamin supplement.

Auntie Shahla's Sfiha
Strudel Pastry Stuffed with Minced Lamb & Sumac

My grandmother Najla was a wonderful cook. She passed down love, courage, strength and most importantly, her passion for cooking, which brought the whole family together. She had nine daughters who all also loved to cook. My Auntie Shahla was the queen of this dish and I was quizzing her about how to make her version of this recipe right up until she passed away in 2009. Although she gave her recipe to me, it never tasted quite the same as hers. Her version was special as she made them as they are made in Yaffa in Palestine and she wanted to carry on this tradition. In other parts of Palestine they are made in a flat, oblong pizza shape, rather than rolled as we do here.

When my granny, aunties and my mum come to visit they always make batches of *sfiha* to put in the freezer so that they can be enjoyed at a later date. Although it may look simple, the actual flattening of the dough and rolling it out to almost paper thin, then folding it like a snail is the tricky part. You don't want it to be too thick otherwise the dough will be too stodgy. It should crisp and flake in your mouth. The main ingredient is sumac, which is a powder of crushed red berries that have a citrus tang to them and a beautiful deep crimson colour; it is used in many other Palestinian dishes, such as *Mussakhan* (see page 156) and *Salatet Fattoush* (see page 112).

Makes 15

750g (1lb 10oz) plain flour
350–550ml (12–19fl oz) water
(depending on weather
conditions and flour)
olive oil, for frying and
kneading
5–6 onions, diced
500g (1lb 2oz) lamb mince
40–50g (1½–1¾oz) sumac
1 teaspoon ground
cinnamon
sea salt and black pepper

Make the dough by putting the flour in an electric mixer with the dough hook fitted and combine with the water – start with 350ml (12fl oz) of the water and add more as necessary until the dough is fully combined and holds its shape. You want a soft dough that holds itself together in a small ball. Cut the dough into 15 balls, lay them out on a well-oiled tray and cover with cling film. Leave to rest for 1 hour.

Meanwhile, make the filling. Heat a little oil in a pan and fry the onions until soft. Add the mince and season to taste. Add the sumac and cinnamon and taste again to check the seasoning. Mix well until everything is brown and the flavour is as you wish. It should taste a little peppery with a gorgeous tang. Leave the meat to cool down before filling the pastry.

Preheat the oven to 220°C fan (240°C/465°F/Gas 9).

Gently flatten and stretch the dough balls into long, thin strips, using olive oil (not flour) to prevent sticking. They should be stretched as thin as possible so that you can practically see through them – it is normal for the dough to break a little, and you can just fold it over on to itself if this happens.

Add a line of filling down one side. Roll the dough over to cover the meat and make a long sausage shape. Swirl the sausage round to make a snail shape. Place them on a baking sheet and bake for 15–20 minutes until lightly golden.

Tip: If you want to make a big batch to be able to keep some in the freezer, cook them for 7–10 minutes, let them cool, then freeze until needed (they will cook from frozen in 7–10 minutes).

Batrakh Ma' Toum Wa Zeit Zeytoun
Grey Mullet Roe with Shaved Garlic & Olive Oil

My parents love this. It took a while to enjoy it as children as we were not used to the unusually strong flavour. But I promise you, it is so, so good and very different to a normal breakfast. It is served as an accompaniment to other dishes, such as *Ful Mudammas* (see below), *M'sabaha* (see page 75) and *Bayd Wa Lahmeh Ma' Salatat Jarjir* (see page 29).

Serves 2

50g (1¾oz) grey mullet roe (found at your local fishmonger)
2 garlic cloves, finely sliced
4 tablespoons olive oil
Khubez (pita bread, see page 48), to serve

Use a very sharp knife to slice the mullet roe into really thin strips at an angle and lay them out on a plate.

Do the same with the garlic and place them on top of the mullet roe, then drizzle with olive oil.

Serve with warm *Khubez* (pita bread) and use them to make little sandwiches with the roe as the filling.

Ful Mudammas
Brown Broad Beans with Lemon, Tomato & Olive Oil

Ful (brown broad beans) are eaten everywhere in the Middle East. This recipe is a wonderful poor man's food that has flavours of earthiness, tang, spice and familiarity – everything that describes Palestine for me. My father is an expert at making this dish. I think the right combination of ingredients is vital otherwise one thing may overpower the others, and the *ful* should be the star here. The origins of *ful* are unknown but there are links dating as far back as 4th-century Egypt; it has been mentioned that the beans were cooked in large pots and buried underground (*mudammas* means 'buried').

Serves 4

2 x 400g (14oz) tins brown broad beans (see page 20)
juice of 2 lemons
2 garlic cloves, chopped
1 green chilli, chopped
1 tomato, diced
a bunch of fresh flat-leaf parsley, roughly chopped
olive oil, to drizzle
sea salt

Empty the beans into a saucepan with the liquid from the tins and heat for about 5 minutes over a high heat, until the beans are thoroughly heated all the way through. Add a little more liquid, if needed, to keep it slightly wet.

Once the beans are warm, crush half of them with a fork, leaving the rest whole. Add the lemon juice, garlic and chilli and mix, adding salt to taste. Top with the tomato and parsley, drizzle with some olive oil and serve.

Tip: Use tinned brown broad (fava) beans if you can find them (sometimes labelled as *Ful Mudammas* in Middle Eastern grocery or online stores as that is what they are mostly used for) or dried brown broad beans or tinned haricot beans.

Fattet' Hummus
Traditional Breakfast Hummus

Fattet Hummus is one of my favourite types of dish – it is warm, hearty, packed with a tangy zing of garlic and brings back the comfort of home every time. This type of dish is usually eaten during Ramadan but it is also often enjoyed for breakfast on a Friday, or for a Sunday lunch. This dish is enjoyed hot and should be eaten as soon as it's made otherwise the bread will go soggy. My mum made this often at home – there was always a scramble to get your spoon in first to make sure you got the crunchy bread at the bottom. But in all honesty the softer bread tastes sublime too – full of the yogurt, lemon and tahini flavour.

Chickpeas are packed with iron, zinc and protein, making them an excellent choice for non meat eaters to get their daily burst of much-needed energy and vitamins.

Serves 6–8

150ml (5fl oz) tahini (see
    page 21)
375ml (13fl oz) Greek yogurt
1 garlic clove, crushed
1 green chilli, finely chopped
juice of 2 lemons
4 *Khubez* (pita bread,
    see page 48), cut into
    diamond shapes
olive oil, for drizzling
a bunch of fresh flat-leaf
    parsley, chopped
paprika, for sprinkling
1 pomegranate, seeded
100g (3½oz) toasted pine
    nuts
sea salt and black pepper
fresh mint leaves, to garnish

For the hummus:
2 x 400g (14oz) tin of
    chickpeas
juice of 2 lemons
1 garlic clove, crushed
2 tablespoons tahini
1 tablespoon Greek yogurt
1 teaspoon sea salt

Preheat the oven to 180°C fan (200°C/400°F/Gas 6).

Mix the tahini with the yogurt, garlic, chilli and lemon juice. Season to taste.

Drizzle the pita bread pieces with oil and place them on a baking tray. Toast in the oven for 12–15 minutes until golden.

Now make the hummus. In a saucepan, warm the chickpeas with the liquid from the tins until they are heated through. Strain, but reserve the cooking liquid. Put half the chickpeas in a blender with the rest of the hummus ingredients and blitz to a smooth paste. Add this to the tahini/yogurt mixture.

Place the toasted bread in a serving bowl, adding 120ml (4fl oz) of the reserved chickpea cooking liquid and three-quarters of the remaining chickpeas. Pour over one-quarter of the hummus and yogurt mix and combine it all together until all of the bread is covered and coated. Top with the rest of the yogurt and hummus mix.

Decorate with chopped parsley, paprika, pomegranate seeds, the remaining chickpeas and the toasted pine nuts. Drizzle with olive oil, garnish with mint and serve.

Tips: Make sure you have all the ingredients prepared and ready before you begin as this dish needs to be put together quite quickly once the bread and liquid have been combined.

I use tinned chickpeas to make this dish faster to prepare as it has so many components to it, but you can use dried chickpeas if preferred (see page 20).

Labneh

Labneh is a strained yogurt often enjoyed in the Middle East. You can buy labneh ready-made in most Middle Eastern shops and, if that fails, some Middle Eastern restaurants will sell it to you. If you don't want to buy it and are feeling a little more adventurous you can make it yourself. In Palestine and the rest of the Middle East, they didn't used to have all the technological equipment that we have now, so cooking techniques had to be easy. This method removes the whey from the yogurt, making it dense and slightly tangy. I love rolling mine into balls and coating with different flavours, but it is also good simply spread on bread and is delicious enjoyed at any time of the day.

Makes 15–20 balls

800g (1lb 12oz) Greek yogurt
1 teaspoon sea salt
olive oil, for storage

To flavour (optional):
za'atar (see page 17)
sumac
dried mint

You will also need:
muslin or kitchen paper

Lay some muslin over a sieve set on top of a bowl, or you can wrap it around a tap to create a hanging nest. If you are using kitchen paper, use 5–6 sheets and lay them in a sieve set over a bowl.

Mix the yogurt with the salt and pour it into the muslin or kitchen paper. Wrap the muslin or kitchen paper around the yogurt and leave it to hang for 24–48 hours so that the liquid can drip away.

After this time, it should be like a thick and creamy paste with a sour taste and a hint of salt. Roll the labneh into 2.5cm (1 inch) balls, and either leave plain, or roll in the separate flavourings until coated. Serve straightaway or you can pack them into an airtight jar, cover with olive oil and store in the fridge.

Tip: You can also use the labneh as a spread, just drizzled with za'atar and some good extra virgin olive oil. Eat with *Khubez* (pita bread, see page 48).

Figs with Labneh & Honey on Toasted Bread

I love this dish as it has the salty-sweet taste that I adore. Using figs is very much a part of daily life in Palestine when they are in season. Luckily, living in London, I can find almost anything from all over the world at any time, so I don't have to miss out on such beauties when I have a yearning for them. This is my equivalent of jam on toast but tastes so much better.

Serves 2

2 slices of sourdough bread
2 labneh balls (see above)
2 ripe figs, sliced
2 tablespoons honey
freshly snipped chives,
   to garnish

Toast your bread, then spread one labneh ball over each piece.

Place the fig slices on top, drizzle with honey and garnish with freshly snipped chives. Serve and enjoy with a cup of fresh mint tea.

Banadora Wa Sumac

Sumac Tomatoes

This tomato dish is quick and easy to make with a real kick to it. The tomatoes balanced by the sumac, mint and pomegranate work really well here and are enjoyed on many a Palestinian table.

Serves 4

3 beef tomatoes
2 teaspoons sumac
1 teaspoon dried mint
1 teaspoon sea salt
a small bunch of fresh mint
½ pomegranate, seeded
4 tablespoons olive oil

Slice the tomatoes and place them on a serving platter. Sprinkle with the sumac, dried mint and salt.

Pick leaves from the bunch of mint and scatter them all over the tomatoes. Top with the pomegranate seeds and drizzle with olive oil before serving.

Feta Bil Furon

Oven-baked Feta Wrapped in Vine Leaves with Spiced Oil

Feta, vine leaves and seasoning are a match made in heaven. This quick and easy to put together dish is simply gorgeous. *Warak inab*, the vine leaf, is an extremely important ingredient in Palestine. I have used it here in a different way to the usual stuffed and slowly cooked vine leaves (see page 128) and given it a new lease of life. I made this version often in my restaurant, Baity Kitchen, and it was always a big hit.

Serves 4

8 vine leaves
4 tablespoons olive oil
300g (10½oz) feta, cut into
   4 pieces
a small bunch of fresh
   flat-leaf parsley
1 red chilli, chopped
1 teaspoon za'atar
   (see page 17)
2 lemons, peeled and sliced
a squeeze of lemon juice

Preheat the oven to 180°C fan (200°C/400°F/Gas 6).

Blanch the vine leaves for 1–2 minutes in a saucepan of boiling water, then drain them on kitchen paper.

Layer the vine leaves in twos on a baking tray and use a pastry brush to brush them with half the olive oil. Place a piece of feta in the centre of each double-layered leaf.

Combine the remaining ingredients in a bowl and spoon some on top of each piece of feta. Wrap the leaves around the feta to lightly seal each parcel. Bake in the oven for 5 minutes until the leaves have dried and curled up. Open up the parcels and eat the feta with the crisped vine leaf and any leaf crumbs that have broken off.

Mana'eesh Za'atar
Fluffy Za'atar Sesame Breakfast Bread

These soft, doughy, pillowy wonders are eaten every single day in Palestine and I try to make them whenever I can. It is such a comforting food that brings back memories of when my family were all together around the kitchen table picking which flavour of bread was our favourite. Mine is a combination of cheese and za'atar, but you can also make them with minced lamb and *kishek* (a powdery cereal of burghul (cracked wheat) fermented with milk and yogurt), which is a very particular flavour. I made these a lot at my restaurant, Baity Kitchen, and they were a firm favourite with my local clients who were Middle Eastern and missing home – it gave me joy to see their faces as they ate them. These are best eaten warm and I promise you, there won't be many left. It takes a bit of time for the rising and baking but is definitely worth it.

Makes 25–35 breads
(depending on size)

525g (1lb 3oz) plain flour
2 tablespoons instant yeast
3 tablespoons dried
  milk powder
2 tablespoons Greek yogurt
2 teaspoons caster sugar
1 teaspoon sea salt
120ml (4fl oz) sunflower oil,
  plus extra for oiling
300ml (10fl oz) warm water

For the topping:
250g (9oz) za'atar
  (see page 17)
400ml (14fl oz) olive oil

Mix 130g (4½oz) of the flour and all the other ingredients together in an electric mixer with the dough hook fitted for 4 minutes. When combined, add the remaining flour and mix again until it comes together into a dough. Turn the dough out onto a floured worktop and knead for 5–7 minutes. Place the dough in a lightly oiled bowl, cover with a clean cloth, then leave it to rise for 1 hour in a warm place.

Cut the dough into 25–35 small balls, place them on a lightly oiled baking tray and leave them to rise again for about 10 minutes. Flatten the balls to make circle shapes.

Preheat the oven to 200°C fan (220°C/425°F/Gas 7).

Mix the topping ingredients together in a bowl and spread or brush the mixture on top of the dough circles. Leave to rest for a final 5–10 minutes.

Place the breads on a baking tray lined with baking parchment (you should fit about 8–10 on each tray, so you may need to cook in batches). Bake for about 10 minutes, or until the base of each bread is slightly browned – the cooking time will depend on their size. These breads will keep for about 2 days if stored in an airtight container.

Tip: You can part-cook these breads for about 5 minutes, place them in the freezer until you need them, then finish baking them in the oven from frozen for 8–10 minutes until slightly browned.

Za'atar Buns

When I first began cooking, I had a thing for baking. I may not have been the best at it but I found it very therapeutic. I also loved changing recipes to make them my own, and as I am more of a savoury person than a sweet one, this za'atar bun recipe was a winner for me. I bought a book by my absolute favourite chef (who actually inspired me to become a chef in the first place), Nigella Lawson's *How to be a Domestic Goddess*. The recipe that stood out for me was the Norwegian Cinnamon Buns. They quickly became a favourite and I made them time and time again, but one day I felt they needed a Palestinian revamp. So I added some more flour, swapped out the sugar and replaced it with za'atar and olive oil and a sprinkling of sesame seeds. These were just heavenly. So huge thanks must go to Nigella for the original inspiration.

Makes 18–21 buns

800g (1lb 12oz) plain flour,
   or more if needed
25g (1oz) caster sugar
2 teaspoons sea salt
21g (¾oz) instant yeast or
   45g (1½oz) fresh yeast
100g (3½oz) butter, melted
400ml (14fl oz) milk, warmed
2 eggs, beaten

For the filling:
150ml (5fl oz) olive oil
175g (6oz) za'atar
   (see page 17)
50g (1¾oz) sesame seeds
1 egg, beaten, to glaze

Preheat the oven to 210°C fan (230°C/455°F/Gas 8). Line a large roasting tin or a 33 x 22cm (13¼ x 8¾ inch) brownie tin with baking parchment.

Mix the flour, sugar, salt and yeast together in a large bowl. Whisk the melted butter into the milk and eggs, then stir this into the flour mixture. Mix to combine, then knead the dough either by hand or using the dough hook of an electric mixer until it is smooth and springy. If it is too wet, simply add a little more flour (I have used up to 1kg/2¼lb flour, depending on the weather).

Form the dough into a ball, place in an oiled bowl, cover with cling film and leave it to rise for about 25 minutes.

Roll out the dough on a lightly floured surface to a rectangle of roughly 50 x 25cm (20 x 10 inches).

Mix the olive oil, za'atar and half the sesame seeds in a small bowl, then spread it over the dough so that it is evenly coated all over.

Roll the dough up from the longest side into a long roll. Cut the roll into about twenty 2cm (1 inch) slices. Sit the slices in the prepared tin, making sure the cut-side is facing up. Don't worry if they don't fit snugly together as they will swell and rise when they prove and bake.

Brush with beaten egg and sprinkle all over with the remaining sesame seeds. Leave them to rise for another 15 minutes to get the best volume on them.

Bake the buns for 20–25 minutes until they have risen and are golden brown. Don't worry if they catch in places. Remove the buns from the tin and leave to cool slightly, before eating them with tomatoes, labneh and feta cheese.

Za'atar Scones

This scone recipe came to me by accident when I was making a large batch of traditional scones for a breakfast with different kinds of fillings and I just could not bear another sweet smell or taste. I had an extra batch that I had whipped up and instead of sweetening it, I added salt to the mixture and decided to make some to dip into olive oil. I made so many that I eventually sent most of them downstairs to my restaurant, Baity Kitchen, and they literally sold out in about half an hour. I was sitting at the counter eating a mixed plate of tomatoes, olives, olive oil, za'atar and mint with two of these scones and some thick yogurt, when customers asked what I was eating and ordered the same. So these became a staple at Baity and in my home. They are super easy to make, cook quickly and have such a wonderful layered texture with a crunchy outside.

Makes 16 large scones

680g (1lb 7oz) plain flour, plus extra for flouring
2 tablespoons sea salt
1½ tablespoons baking powder
¾ teaspoon bicarbonate of soda
250g (9oz) cold butter, cut into cubes
480ml (15fl oz) buttermilk (or yogurt)
2 big handfuls of za'atar (see page 17)
1 egg, beaten

Preheat the oven to 190°C fan (210°C/415°F/Gas 6–7).

Put the flour, salt, baking powder and bicarbonate of soda in a bowl and mix together. Add the butter and mix again to create a crumbly effect but not like that of crumble – you want to be able to see bits of butter in the mixture.

Add the buttermilk and combine. Once this has been mixed, tip the dough out onto a lightly floured, cold surface, add the za'atar and knead it for a minute or two to make a ball, but try not to over-knead.

Cut the dough in half. Roll each half out to about 2cm (¾ inch) thick and cut out 8 equal-sized pieces (with a cutter or by hand) to make a total of 16 scones. Remember these will double in size in the oven.

Brush the scones with beaten egg and bake for 18–25 minutes until golden.

Tip: The scone recipe I use is a basic one – you can add 100g (3½oz) caster sugar instead of salt and up to 150–200g (5–7oz) chocolate or dates to make this into a sweet recipe (see page 227).

Khubez
Pita bread

Is there anything more satisfying than making your own bread? I think not. Auntie Dunia is the pastry queen in my family and this is her recipe. We eat this type of bread all over the Middle East. The breads can vary in thickness but generally this is our staple version. I love eating pita with everything because it is light and doesn't overpower any dish. This recipe is extremely easy to make and can easily be doubled to make a larger quantity. Keep an eye on the breads during baking – don't bake for too long otherwise the breads will be too crunchy and lose their softness.

Serves 8

7g (⅓oz) instant yeast

240ml (8¼fl oz) tepid/warm water

1 teaspoon golden caster sugar

400g (14oz) plain flour

50ml (2fl oz) olive oil, plus extra for oiling

Mix the yeast and warm water together in a large bowl. Leave for a couple of minutes and then add the sugar and stir through. Add the flour and olive oil and knead together until you have a smooth doughy consistency that bounces back. This should take 5–8 minutes. Leave the dough in an oiled bowl for about 1 hour until it has risen.

Preheat the oven to 220°C fan (240°C/465°F/Gas 9).

Once risen, cut the dough into 8 equal pieces and shape them into nice balls. Lay them on a baking tray and leave to rise for another 10 minutes. Once risen, flatten each ball with a rolling pin (not too thin), lay on a baking sheet and bake for 5 minutes or until the pitas have puffed up.

Serve, dipping into some olive oil and za'atar if liked. These will keep for a few days if sealed in an airtight container.

Ka'ak Al-Quds
Palestinian Sesame Handbag Bread

This classic, iconic bread is sold everywhere in Palestine – on the streets, in every bakery and by men shouting down the streets of Jerusalem informing everyone that they are coming with *ka'ak* bread. It is similar to the *khubez* (pita bread, see page 48) but with the addition of yogurt and milk and is traditionally eaten with a pot of fresh mint tea, or simply stuffed with cheese and za'atar – that's how I like mine. The breads are cooked in an extremely hot oven to create the pocket in the middle. It is also good eaten with honey and jams for a sweeter taste.

Makes 12–16 breads

500ml (18fl oz) water
150ml (5fl oz) milk
150ml (5fl oz) Greek yogurt
14g (½oz) instant yeast
2 tablespoons golden caster sugar
1 tablespoon sea salt
2 tablespoons olive oil
1.1kg (2lb 7oz) plain flour
1 egg, for brushing
150–200g (5–7oz) sesame seeds

Warm the water in a saucepan over a gentle heat – it should be slightly warmer than body temperature so that it can have an effect on the yeast. Add the milk and warm it through too. Don't overheat the liquid otherwise it will kill the growth in the yeast and ruin the final result.

Place the warm water and milk in a bowl and stir through the yogurt. Add the yeast, giving it a little stir. Add all the remaining ingredients, except the egg and sesame seeds, and begin to combine it together into a dough. Knead for about 5–8 minutes depending on the flour, weather and other elements. When the dough feels ready – it should have a slight bounce when you touch it – turn it out into a well-oiled bowl and cover it. Leave it to rise for about 2 hours in a warm place.

Knock back the air from the risen dough, then cut it into 12–16 equal-sized pieces. Roll each piece into a ball, place them on lightly oiled baking trays and leave to rise for about 30 minutes. Preheat the oven to its highest temperature – about 220°C fan (240°C/465°F/Gas 9).

Lightly flour the worktop. Roll each piece of dough into a teardrop shape that is not too thin. Cut out a circular shape (I used a small upturned cup to get the right size and shape) from the narrower top end of each bread and brush egg wash over the surface. Sprinkle all over with sesame seeds.

The breads will need to be cooked one at a time. Lay one bread on a baking tray and bake for 10–15 minutes. It is important to use your own judgement here as all ovens vary – keep checking the breads during baking and take them out when they have turned golden brown and have puffed up. The baked breads will keep for a day or two if stored in an airtight container.

Hearty Pulses & Grains

Wheat, rice, pulses and grains are staple ingredients in the Middle East and are the basis of a Middle Eastern diet, both historically and today. Grains such as burghul, freekeh and couscous come from wheat and are used in many Palestinian dishes. Wonderful varieties of chickpeas, lentils, broad beans, and many more kinds of pulses are also widely enjoyed. The number of dishes that can be made using these ingredients can fill a whole book in itself – cold, hot, in a stew, salad, main course or starter, they can be used everywhere. The cost of these products is also why they are so popular. Palestine doesn't have a thriving economy like Western countries, with most people living very humble lives, so the price of ingredients has to be low. Once you try these dishes you will understand why they have been so popular for such a long time.

Shorabet Freekeh
Freekeh Soup

Freekeh (toasted, cracked green wheat) soup is one of my favourites. In my family, we usually eat this during Ramadan to break our fast, but it is good to eat all year round. It has a beautiful nutty flavour that tastes as if it is incredibly good for you. The nutritional benefits of freekeh are endless – it is low in fat, high in fibre, packed full of zinc, calcium and iron and contains twice as much protein as quinoa. It is also lower in the glycemic index making it great for weight loss and for people trying to control their blood sugar. Freekeh is a centuries-old grain, which packs a much-needed health boost. You can omit the chicken from this recipe if you prefer, to make a wonderful vegetarian soup.

Serves 6

1 small chicken, weighing about 1.2kg (2lb 12oz)

2 onions, 1 quartered and 1 finely chopped

4 cardamom pods

1 bay leaf

2 tablespoons sea salt, plus extra to season the soup

1.5 litres (2½ pints) water

100ml (3½fl oz) vegetable oil

275g (9¾oz) smooth freekeh

1 teaspoon ground cinnamon

1 teaspoon ground nutmeg

1 teaspoon black pepper

Greek yogurt, to serve

Put the chicken in a saucepan with the quartered onion, cardamom, bay leaf, salt and water. Bring to the boil and continue cooking for 45 minutes.

Remove the chicken from the saucepan, reserving the broth, and use a slotted spoon to lift out the onion, spices and bay leaf. Leave the chicken to cool a little and then shred the meat.

Heat the oil in a saucepan and sauté the chopped onion until it is golden. Add the freekeh and stir it through the onions.

Add the reserved chicken broth to the freekeh and onions and boil for about 20–25 minutes (this will add a huge amount of flavour to the freekeh as it cooks). Keep stirring as it cooks or the freekeh may catch on the base of the saucepan.

Once the soup is smooth and of a consistency to your liking, add the shredded chicken and stir through. Pour into serving bowls and season with a sprinkling of cinnamon, nutmeg and some salt and black pepper. Serve with some cool thick yogurt and, if you like, some thin toasted *Khubez* (pita bread, see page 48) to dip into the soup.

Tips: If you can't find smooth freekeh, you can pulse coarse freekeh in a high-speed blender until it is partly smooth – you want to stop before it has become a stodgy paste as that won't be good for cooking with.

If the soup thickens too much, simply add more stock or water to loosen it (this can often happen as freekeh absorbs liquid very well).

Fil Fil Mahshi Bil Freekeh

Freekeh-stuffed Peppers

My mother used to make many versions of stuffed peppers, one of which involved freekeh. That is the version I have reproduced here, adapted to my taste. I had many vegetarian customers at my restaurant who loved the variety of my dishes. There were over 20 different options on the menu and this one became a really big hit. It is hearty, punchy, fresh and filling. The tomato sauce that the freekeh is cooked in gives it a gentle flavour and a dollop of gorgeous thick Greek yogurt on the side really makes this a go-to dish when you are feeling hungry and worn down. I made hundreds of these a week at the restaurant and always had people commenting on how this tasted like home. Home to them could be America, France, Italy, the Middle East, Asia – it didn't matter what they were eating, but the essence of home was felt in the food, and that has always been my aim.

Serves 4

2 red peppers, halved lengthways and deseeded
1 small courgette, chopped
1 spring onion, diced
½ onion, diced
2 small tomatoes, diced
100g (3½oz) coarse freekeh
500ml (18fl oz) tomato passata
2 teaspoons sea salt
1 teaspoon black pepper
50ml (2fl oz) olive oil
a bunch of fresh flat-leaf parsley, chopped
a small bunch of fresh chives

Preheat the oven to 190°C fan (210°C/415°F/Gas 6–7). Place the cut peppers in a deep baking tray.

Mix the remaining vegetables with the freekeh in a large bowl and add half the passata. Season with half the salt and the pepper and stir through the olive oil and herbs. Use a spoon to fill the pepper halves with the mixture.

Pour the rest of the passata around the peppers in the tray, adding about 360ml (12¼fl oz) water and season with the remaining salt. Cover the tray tightly with foil – this will create steam inside to cook the freekeh. Bake for about 35 minutes until the freekeh is cooked. Use a small teaspoon to try a bit of freekeh; if it needs more time, return the tray to the oven for another 5–10 minutes.

Serve with some of the warm tomato passata from the baking tray and a dollop of Greek yogurt.

Tip: If you have any stuffing mixture left over (which I always do as all peppers are different sizes), simply place it in a saucepan, add enough water to cover by 2.5cm (1 inch) and cook over a medium heat for 15 minutes to make a lovely thick, grainy soup.

Salatet Djaj Wa Freekeh
Freekeh Salad with Marinated Chicken & Pomegranate Dressing

This dish is what dreams are made of. Freekeh, which is a toasted, cracked green wheat, is simply heavenly. It is used in so many ways and is so good for you. I made this dish many times at my restaurant, Baity Kitchen, I almost couldn't keep up with myself. The crunchy nuttiness of the wheat contrasts with the sweet, succulent creamy chicken, herby salad and the sharpness of the dressing. It is a combination of ingredients that I would choose to eat as my last meal on earth.

Serves 4–6

300g (10½oz) coarse freekeh

4 chicken breasts, cut in half
   lengthways

1 tablespoon dried mint

1 tablespoon za'atar
   (see page 17)

1 teaspoon dried chilli flakes

4 tablespoons pomegranate
   molasses

olive oil, for drizzling

a large bunch of fresh
   flat-leaf parsley, chopped

5 spring onions, chopped

a bunch of fresh chives,
   chopped

1 pomegranate, seeded

a bunch of rocket

2 red chillies, chopped

sea salt and black pepper

For the dressing:

100ml (3½fl oz) apple cider
   vinegar

4 tablespoons pomegranate
   molasses

1 large tablespoon golden
   caster sugar

juice of 2 lemons

180ml (6fl oz) extra virgin
   olive oil

1 tablespoon dried mint

1 tablespoon za'atar

1 teaspoon sea salt

Boil the freekeh in a saucepan of salted water for about 30 minutes. Check to see if it needs longer as the grain tends to come in different sizes. Remove the pan from the heat, drain and then leave the freekeh to cool down slightly. I like to keep it a little warm so that it soaks up the flavour of the dressing.

Preheat the oven to 190°C fan (210°C/415°F/Gas 6–7).

Put the chicken in a bowl and add the dried mint, za'atar, chilli flakes, pomegranate molasses, a drizzle of olive oil and season with some salt and black pepper. Mix to ensure it is all coated. Tip the chicken out onto a baking tray, pouring over any excess juices from the bowl as you do. Bake for about 20–25 minutes until cooked through. Slice the chicken into strips lengthways.

Add the parsley, spring onion and chives to the freekeh and mix together. Add the pomegranate seeds, sliced chicken and its juices, the rocket and red chilli and mix well.

Mix the dressing ingredients together and toss them through the salad. Serve this salad in a beautiful bowl, as this dish really deserves it. Add a bit more salt or sugar or whatever seasoning you prefer – it should be made to your taste, but you are aiming for something tangy, sweet and spicy.

Tip: Middle Eastern rocket, *jarjir*, is bigger, less tough and slightly more peppery than other varieties – you can get leaves that are half the size of your palm! This is the best kind to use if you can find it, but normal rocket is fine if not.

Adas Wa Ruz / Shorabet Adas
Cumin-infused Lentil Stew & Soup (two-in-one)

The history of lentils goes all the way back to the Bible, when Jacob purchases Esau's birthright with a bowl of stewed lentils. They are also symbolic to Jews in mourning – they represent the birth and death of life due to their circular and unbroken shape. In Ancient Greece, poets wrote about lentils being the 'sweetest of delicacies', so Middle Easterners are not alone in their praise for this humble pulse. I think lentils are so versatile and tasty. The dish I make is simply lentils with rice and cumin. You get two dishes in one when you strain the liquid out of the lentils to make a soup.

Cumin is very important in this dish as it is known to prevent flatulence, which is handy as lentils can make you a little gassy – so be careful! Cumin is the second most popular spice in the world after pepper and is very versatile. It also has a large percentage of iron, which is great in combination with this lentil dish. It is said to be good for treating the effects of a common cold and can help with stomach pain – although this may not be scientific fact, from personal experience, I'm sure there is some truth to it.

Serves 6–8

150ml (5fl oz) olive oil
2 large onions, sliced into
    half moons
a large bunch of fresh
    flat-leaf parsley, roughly
    chopped
480ml (17½fl oz) chicken
    stock
500g (1lb 2oz) red split lentils
100g (3½oz) basmati rice
2–3 large tablespoons
    ground cumin
sea salt

To serve:
croutons, radish, spring
    onions, lemons and
    Tabasco sauce
Khubez (pita bread, see
    page 48)

Heat some of the oil in a frying pan and gently fry the onions until they are caramelized. Use a slotted spoon to remove them from the pan and set aside.

Add the parsley to the pan with a little more olive oil and fry over a high heat until the parsley has crisped up. Be careful as the parsley will pop in the pan as it cooks.

Put the stock in a medium saucepan and add the lentils, rice, 2 tablespoons of the cumin and half the fried onion and fried parsley (reserving the rest for a garnish). You need the stock to sit about 1.5cm (1 inch) above the ingredients, so top up with a little water if needed. Season with salt.

Simmer for 20 minutes. Keep checking the water as lentils soak up a lot as they cook, so you may need to keep topping the liquid up. This extra liquid will make the soup version of this lovely dish so don't worry if there is a lot left at the end.

Once cooked, strain the lentils into another saucepan or bowl – this liquid is your soup. Add 2 ladles of the strained lentils to the soup to thicken and some more cumin if liked. Blitz with a handheld blender just to break up the lentils a little. Keep the soup warm while you arrange the drained lentils.

Put the drained lentils in a serving dish and sprinkle with the remaining onions and parsley.

Serve the soup, garnished with croutons, together with the lentils on the side and accompany both dishes with radish, spring onions, lemon, tabasco and *Khubez* (pita bread).

Rummaniyeh

Lentil & Aubergine Stew with Pomegranate Molasses

My grandmother Najla was born in Yaffa in Palestine and lived there until she met my grandfather Fouad and then moved to Al-Lydd. She has provided my whole family with some really wonderful memories, mainly around food and cooking, as that was what she spent most of her time doing. Her commitment and love to us all has inspired many a chef in our family. This dish is very typical of both Yaffa and Al-Lydd in Palestine and it has become very popular in Gaza, too. So this recipe is dedicated to all those areas where devoted families have continued the traditions that have been passed onto the likes of me, and hopefully now, to you. *Rummaniyeh* means 'pomegranatey'. There are pomegranate seeds and pomegranate molasses all over this dish, draped over lentils and aubergine to create a tangy, earthy combination of utter goodness. A vegan dream!

Serves 4

250g (9oz) brown lentils

1 heaped tablespoon
    ground cumin

600ml (1 pint) water

1 aubergine, peeled and
    cubed into small pieces

1 tablespoon sea salt

50ml (2fl oz) olive oil, plus
    extra for drizzling

4–6 large garlic cloves,
    crushed

150ml (5fl oz) pomegranate
    molasses

juice of 2 lemons

1 pomegranate, seeded

fresh flat-leaf parsley,
    chopped, to garnish

Taboon bread or *Khubez*
    (pita bread, see page 48),
    to serve

Put the lentils, cumin and water in a saucepan, bring to the boil and then continue to boil for 10 minutes. Add the aubergine, salt and leave to simmer while you cook the garlic.

Set another pan over a medium heat. Add the olive oil and the crushed garlic and cook for a few minutes until they turn golden.

When the lentils and aubergine have been cooking for about 25 minutes, add the fried garlic and the pomegranate molasses and mix together. Cook for another 5 minutes, then stir through the lemon juice.

Place in a serving bowl, drizzle with a little olive oil, scatter the pomegranate seeds over the top and finish with some parsley. Enjoy with hot taboon bread (see below) or *Khubez* (pita bread, see page 48).

Tip: Taboon bread is a type of flat bread traditionally baked in a tabun oven and is soft, slightly chewy and doesn't tear easily. It is sold as street food, stuffed with hummus, falafel or shaved meat and is a staple bread in Middle Eastern cuisine.

Salatet Adas Wa Halloumi Mashwi

Lentil & Beetroot Salad with Parsley & Sumac Dressing & Grilled Halloumi

Using lentils in Palestinian cooking is common place – there are so many variations that I could probably dedicate an entire book to the subject. My mother was very creative in the kitchen and, like me, most of what she learned was passed down by her mother, Najla, or was inspired by the desire to recreate dishes she loved. I find cooking very therapeutic and often cook certain dishes when I miss my mum or when I think of my brother and sisters, or a particular moment in time. This is a dish that my mother would make while remembering her childhood, when her mother would make a hearty salad that would fill up her eleven children with utter goodness and plenty of flavour.

Serves 4

2 large beetroot, scrubbed and washed, skin on

2 tablespoons olive oil

200g (7oz) Puy lentils

1 onion, diced

1 x 200g (7oz) pack of halloumi cheese, cut lengthways

sea salt

2 preserved lemons, cut into wedges, to garnish

For the dressing:

150ml (5fl oz) olive oil

1 teaspoon sumac

2 tablespoons white wine vinegar

a bunch of fresh flat-leaf parsley, chopped

1 tablespoon sea salt

juice of 1 lemon

Preheat the oven to 200°C fan (220°C/425°F/Gas 7). Salt the beetroot, drizzle with olive oil and place them on a baking tray lined with baking parchment. Roast them for about 30–40 minutes depending on how large your beetroot are – you don't want them mushy, they should be firm to soft so you don't lose the texture.

Put the lentils and onions in a saucepan of water and bring to the boil. Don't add salt at this stage. Continue cooking for 25–30 minutes, but check after 20 minutes to see how they are doing – I like mine slightly al dente – and add a little salt if needed. Remove the lentils from the heat, drain and leave them to cool slightly.

Make the dressing by mixing all the ingredients together in a small bowl or jar. If you like it more salted, or more vinegary, then please add more. Everything should be slightly tangy as it will penetrate the beetroot and lentils and create a delicious flavour.

When the beetroot is done, remove from the oven, place under cool running water and begin to peel them – the skin should come off quite easily, but if it doesn't, use a knife to help scrape it off. Cut the beetroot into wedges and mix with the lentils. Add the dressing and mix thoroughly.

Heat a frying pan over a high heat and sear the halloumi for 1–2 minutes on each side. You don't need any oil for this – the cheese won't stick or melt – it will become soft and charred and retain a gorgeous pattern. Cut the halloumi into smaller bite-sized pieces and mix some into the salad. Scatter the rest of the halloumi on top and add the preserved lemon and serve.

Mujadarra
Cumin Lentils & Rice with Caramelized Onions

Mujadarra is an all-time favourite in my family. It is hearty and punchy and very filling. The lentils are cooked in water infused with cumin and added to caramelized onions and rice to make this earthy and satisfying dish. I eat this all the time with a chilli, garlic and tomato salsa on the side to elevate it to another level. There are many different versions of this dish but I think simplicity is key. My mother often also adds lemon juice and rocket for colour and texture.

Serves 4–8

400g (14oz) brown lentils

2 tablespoons ground cumin

700ml (1¼ pints) water

1 tablespoon olive oil

1 teaspoon ground coriander

1 teaspoon coriander seeds

200g (7oz) basmati or Egyptian rice

200ml (7fl oz) sunflower oil

3 large onions, cut in half and sliced

juice of 2–3 lemons

100ml (3½fl oz) olive oil, for drizzling

30g (1¼oz) rocket or mixed leaves

1 pomegranate, seeded

sea salt

Boil the lentils, cumin and water with 1 teaspoon salt in a saucepan for about 15–20 minutes until they are al dente. Keep checking as you don't want it to turn to mush. Drain, reserving the water, and set aside.

Heat the olive oil in a saucepan over medium heat and fry the ground coriander and coriander seeds for a minute or two. Add the reserved cooking water from the lentils, the rice and 1 tablespoon salt. Bring to the boil and cook for about 5 minutes over a high heat, then reduce the heat to low and cook for another 10–13 minutes.

Heat the sunflower oil in a frying pan and cook the onions until they are caramelized and sticky. Set a few spoonfuls of the onions aside to use as a garnish and then combine the rest with the lentils and rice, making sure you get a nice even mix of everything. Add the lemon juice and a drizzle of olive oil while everything is still warm as it soaks up more of the flavours. I also add salt at this point to make sure that everything is seasoned well.

Add the rocket and pomegranate seeds, mix them through, then garnish with the reserved onions. This dish can be eaten warm or cold and is even good the next day.

Tip: This dish is also delicious served with the salsa on page 24.

Maftoul Tabbouleh
Palestinian Pearl Cous Cous Tabbouleh

Tabbouleh is usually made up of burghul (cracked wheat), parsley, tomatoes, cucumber, spring onions, lemon juice and olive oil, but as my mother used to feel bloated after eating burghul, she decided to leave it out. You must cut the tomatoes and spring onions into really small and equal-sized pieces to make a good tabbouleh otherwise it is just a chopped salad. I love tabbouleh served with crisp romaine lettuce and chillies, but wanted to make it more of a main meal instead of an accompaniment to something, so I added *maftoul* (Palestinian pearl cous cous, see page 17), which gives it a hearty, satisfying feel. It is one of those dishes that is found in every restaurant, home, coffee shop and deli in Palestine and also over here in the UK. It is simple, fresh, tangy, livens the taste buds and awakens the mouth.

Serves 4–6

450g (1lb) *maftoul*
    (Palestinian pearl cous
    cous)
700ml (1¼ pints) water
5 tomatoes
a bunch of spring onions
a large bunch of fresh
    flat-leaf parsley
juice of 3 lemons
1 tablespoon sea salt
olive oil

To serve (optional):
cos or Romaine lettuce
    leaves
1 chopped green chilli

Begin by boiling the *maftoul* and the water in a saucepan for 25–30 minutes, until it has just passed the al dente stage. Remove and rinse under cold water, drain and set aside.

Meanwhile, chop the tomatoes and spring onions into small equal-sized pieces. Chop the parsley until it is small but don't overdo it, as you don't want to bruise the leaves.

Mix all the chopped ingredients together in a bowl. Add the lemon juice, salt and olive oil to taste. This salad should be sharp and tangy to contrast against the creaminess of the *maftoul* and there should be plenty of parsley mixed through (it is essentially a parsley salad).

Enjoy the tabbouleh with fresh crisp lettuce leaves and if you like, as I do, add some chopped green chilli to bring out the flavour.

Maftoul

Palestinian Pearl Cous Cous with Caraway, Chicken, Onions & Parsley

Maftoul is a Palestinian cous cous that has its origins in North Africa. Its name there is *moghrabiyeh*, which refers to the area of the Maghreb (North African countries such as Egypt and Libya etc.). *Maftoul* is also an Arabic word derived from the root 'fa-ta-la', which means 'to roll or to twist', as the grains are actually hand-rolled balls (traditionally by Palestinian housewives), unlike other varieties of cous cous that are made in a factory. They are basically semolina balls that are hardened and cooked like rice and flavoured with the stock or water that they are being cooked in (otherwise they can get a little boring). When I was growing up my mother rarely made the same thing twice within short periods of time and it always surprised me just how many different dishes she could make to feed us all. She didn't make this dish often enough and I'm not sure why because it is so wonderful and has everything in it – flavour, texture and deliciousness.

Serves 2–4

1 whole spatchcocked
   chicken or 2–4
   spatchcocked poussin
olive oil
3 tablespoons ground
   caraway
3 onions, 2 quartered and
   1 chopped
300g (10½oz) *maftoul*
   (Palestinian pearl cous
   cous)
650ml (22fl oz) chicken stock
1 tablespoon caraway seeds
1 x 400g (14oz) tin of
   chickpeas
a bunch of fresh flat-leaf
   parsley, chopped
sea salt and black pepper
Greek yogurt, to serve

Preheat the oven to 190°C fan (210°C/415°F/Gas 6–7).

Rub the chicken or poussin with olive oil and 2 tablespoons of the ground caraway so that it is evenly coated. Put in a roasting dish with the quartered onions and season all over with salt and pepper. Bake for 45–60 minutes if using chicken, or 35–40 minutes if using poussin.

Put the *maftoul* in a saucepan with the chicken stock and 1 tablespoon salt. Bring to the boil over a high heat and cook for 20 minutes. Drain, reserving the stock, then transfer to a bowl and set aside.

Heat some olive oil in the same pan and fry the chopped onion with the remaining ground caraway and the caraway seeds until the onion has softened. Tip in the *maftoul* and the chickpeas and add about 150ml (5fl oz) of the reserved chicken stock. Cook for 5 minutes to heat everything through.

Spoon onto a serving plate or bowl and top with the chicken and some parsley. Serve with yogurt.

Tip: You may need to increase the quantity of spices depending on the size of your chicken or poussin.

Auntie Dunia's Falafel with Tarator Sauce

If you have not eaten a falafel, then I wonder if you have been living on another planet. It is something not to be missed. Falafels are filled with so much goodness that it is almost a crime not to try this recipe. The combination of chickpeas, coriander, garlic, parsley and olive oil is so divine, and to top it all off you can dip it into a tahini sauce, which just adds to the gorgeous taste of this dish. In Palestine, street stalls making and selling falafel are everywhere; vendors cook them on the spot with their scoop and hot oil, and wrap them in flat bread with pickles and tahini. They are devoured as quickly as they are made. It is such a symbol of the Middle East and really reminds me of my family's home.

The chickpea is obviously the star of the show, being full of iron, zinc, dietary fibre and protein. Tahini also has its health benefits – sesame seeds are full of iron, calcium, vitamin B and E and antioxidants. It is also thought that sesame reduces blood cholesterol and when sesame is pulverized into a paste, as with tahini, its nutrients become more active.

Makes 24–30 falafel

400g (14oz) dried chickpeas

2 heaped teaspoons baking powder

a bunch of fresh flat-leaf parsley

a bunch of fresh coriander

2 tablespoons ground coriander

½ onion

1 tablespoon sea salt

a pinch of black pepper

4 garlic cloves, smashed

900ml (1⅔ pints) sunflower or vegetable oil, for frying

2 tablespoons sesame seeds

olive oil, for binding

For the tarator sauce:

8 tablespoons tahini (see page 21)

3 tablespoons Greek yogurt

juice of 3 lemons

1 tablespoon sea salt

First, soak the chickpeas in water with half the baking powder for up to 8 hours – this is best done overnight so you don't have to wait for it. When ready, drain the water and tip the chickpeas into a food processor or blender with the remaining baking powder.

Add the rest of the ingredients, except the sunflower oil and sesame seeds, to the food processor or blender with enough olive oil to bind the mixture together. The olive oil will help make the mixture workable, but don't add too much – start with 50ml (2fl oz) and add more if needed as you don't want the mixture to be too wet. Blitz until you have formed a paste.

Begin shaping your falafel into balls, making sure you leave the bottoms flat so they can stand up. Sprinkle the falafel with sesame seeds and press them gently to help the seeds stick.

Heat the sunflower or vegetable oil in a pan over a high heat until very hot. Fry the falafel in batches of 4–5 at a time in the hot oil for 6–8 minutes, until cooked all the way through. Turn the falafel occasionally as they are cooking so that they turn an even chocolate-brown colour all over.

To make the tahini sauce, mix all the ingredients together and add a little water if necessary to loosen – you are looking for quite a runny consistency.

Enjoy the falafels by drizzling them with creamy tahini sauce and eat while still warm.

Tip: Always use dried chickpeas for this recipe – tinned chickpeas are too waterlogged and will not form the shape required and will break when frying.

M'sabaha

Warm Chunky Chickpeas with Cumin, Garlic & Yogurt

If you love chickpeas, you will fall in love with this dish over and over again. It is a better, tastier dish than hummus, in my opinion, with the hint of cumin creating a dreamy sense of home and comfort.

Serves 4–6

1 x 400g (14oz) tin of chickpeas

2 garlic cloves, finely chopped

1½ tablespoons ground cumin

3 tablespoons tahini

2 tablespoons Greek yogurt

juice of 1 lemon

4 tablespoons olive oil

1 green chilli, diced (optional)

sea salt

fresh parsley and paprika, to garnish

Pour the chickpeas and the liquid from the tin into a saucepan. Set over a medium-low heat and simmer gently for 5 minutes. Add the garlic and cumin and cook for a further 5 minutes.

In a separate bowl, mix the tahini, yogurt, lemon juice, olive oil, chilli, if using, and some salt together. Add this to the chickpea mix and stir together.

Remove three-quarters of the mixture, then use a handheld blender to pulverize what is left in the pan. Add the removed whole chickpeas back to the mix and stir through to create a chunkier texture. Check for taste and add more lemon, salt or chilli if needed.

Transfer to a serving dish, sprinkle with some parsley and paprika and serve with bread.

Tip: You could use dried chickpeas (see page 20) here, but to make a quick dip it's easier to use tinned.

Spiced Chickpeas

I have recently discovered these gorgeously crunchy, spiced chickpeas that are super easy to make and taste divine. You can change up the spices every time you make this to create a different snack each time.

Serves 6–8

300g (10½oz) dried chickpeas

1 teaspoon cayenne pepper

1 teaspoon smoked paprika

1 teaspoon za'atar (see page 17)

1 teaspoon ground cumin

olive oil, for drizzling

sea salt

Soak the chickpeas in a bowl of water overnight.

The next day, preheat the oven to 200°C fan (220°C/425°F/Gas 7). Rinse the soaked chickpeas to get rid of all the starch and spread them out on a baking tray. Sprinkle with the spices and add the oil and some salt. Toss together so the chickpeas are well coated.

Bake for 35–40 minutes, turning every 15 minutes. Leave to cool and harden and become crunchy, then serve or store in an airtight container for 2–3 days.

Tip: It is important to use dried chickpeas (see page 20) here as the tinned ones are too soft and waterlogged and will not harden properly when baked in the oven.

Teta Najla's Besara
Ancient Broad Bean & Jute Mallow Dip

Besara, a delicious broad bean dip, is an almost forgotten Palestinian dish, but through this book and thanks to wonderful up-and-coming Palestinian chefs, we are giving it a new lease of life. It is originally an Egyptian dish from the Pharaonic times. It then travelled to Palestine and was changed to accommodate the style of cooking there. It is also very popular in Egypt, but we make ours differently with the use of *molokhia* (the leaves of the Corchorus plant also known as jute mallow), which is a must (see page 158). In Egypt they use more green herbs and spices, which is equally delicious but not quite the same as the Palestinian version. My Auntie Lamia is famous for making this in our family as she and my grandmother Najla love it so much.

Serves 4

250g (9oz) dried broad
    beans
100ml (3½fl oz) olive oil, plus
    extra for drizzling
1 large onion, cut in half,
    then sliced
5 garlic cloves, crushed
150g (5½oz) dried *molokhia*
    (jute mallow)
1 tablespoon ground cumin
1 tablespoon ground
    coriander
1 tablespoon sea salt
1 lemon, for squeezing
1 red chilli, finely chopped

Soak the dried beans in a bowl of water overnight. Drain and rinse, then drain again before using.

Put the soaked beans in a large saucepan of water, bring to the boil, then continue to boil for about 30 minutes.

Heat the olive oil in a frying pan and fry the onions and garlic until golden. Set aside.

When the beans have cooked and softened, you should have only half the water volume left in the pan. Add the *molokhia* (jute mallow), cumin, coriander and salt and mix together. Add half the fried onions and mix through. Use a handheld blender to purée the mixture. Taste for seasoning and add more salt if needed.

Transfer to a serving bowl, drizzle over some olive oil, squeeze over the lemon juice and garnish with chillies and the remaining fried onion.

Tips: This is best eaten warm but is perfectly delicious cold. I like to eat mine with taboon bread (see page 64), which is similar to naan bread.

You can use frozen chopped *molokhia* (jute mallow) if you can't find dried *molokhia*.

I have also made this with chickpeas when I have run out of broad beans. It works perfectly well and is equally delicious, though it creates a completely different dish in flavour.

Kubbeh Bil Sanniyeh
Burghul (Cracked Wheat) & Spiced Minced Lamb Pie

Kubbeh Bil Sanniyeh is eaten in my household with a big dollop of my mother's *Mutabbal* (see page 102) – without it, it just doesn't seem to work. The burghul (cracked wheat) is what makes this dish stand out from a normal kufta as it changes the texture completely and makes it more rigid and cake-like. It is made with a certain amount of delicate spices that are carefully selected to season it in just the right way. This is an easy dish to make but it is difficult to master the art of the design on top. Usually the pattern is a diamond shape, but in Palestine the shapes can vary between different families and areas of the country.

Serves 8–12

For the *haswheh* (stuffing):
200ml (7fl oz) sunflower oil
8 onions, finely chopped or minced
1kg (2¼lb) lamb mince
2 teaspoons black pepper
1 teaspoon ground cinnamon
2 teaspoons dried marjoram
sea salt

For the topping and base:
1kg (2¼lb) fine burghul (cracked wheat)
1.5kg (3lb 5oz) lamb mince
1 onion, cut into quarters
1 teaspoon ground cinnamon
1 teaspoon ground cumin
1 teaspoon black pepper
1 small green chilli, chopped
2–3 sprigs of fresh mint leaves, chopped
3 teaspoons dried marjoram
olive oil, for greasing and drizzling

First, make the *haswheh* (stuffing). Heat the sunflower oil in a large pan and sauté the onions until softened. Sauté the lamb in a separate pan, then mix together with the onions. Add the black pepper, cinnamon, marjoram and some salt to taste. Stir and cook until mixed, then leave it to cool slightly.

Next, make the top and bottom layers. Wash the burghul (cracked wheat), soak it in water for 5–10 minutes, then drain. Add the lamb. Purée the onion in a food processor and mix it with the burghul and lamb. Add the spices and herbs, mix together, then grind the mixture in a meat grinder, food processor or high-speed blender until it becomes like a paste or dough.

Preheat the oven to 190°C fan (210°C/415°F/Gas 6–7) and grease either one 37cm (14½ inch) or two 32cm (12 inch) round baking tins with olive oil.

Divide the dough mix in half. Place between two layers of cling film and roll the dough out evenly and smoothly into a circle large enough for your tin or dish. Use cold water to press the meat dough down and spread it into a flat shape. It may be easier to make several small balls, then press them into the tin rather than making one big flat circular shape as it can break easily.

Add the stuffing mix and spread it out to cover the base mixture. Top with the rest of the dough mix and spread so that the stuffing is all covered. Keep using cold water to moisten your fingers while making this to prevent it from sticking. The top layer should be just slightly thicker than the bottom.

Now the fun starts! Make a small incision in the centre to allow some steam out while it cooks and begin by cutting a pattern into the burghul lamb mix (see image). Drizzle 240ml (8fl oz) olive oil over the top, then bake for 45 minutes, depending on how crispy you like it. Alternatively, you can place it in the freezer at this stage (before baking) until you are ready to cook it.

Tips: This is best served with *Mama's Mutabbal* (see page 102) or with a fresh yogurt, cucumber and dried mint dip.

This recipe will make 2 tins (or 3–4 smaller tins) – it's always best to make a few of these, as they are time consuming but definitely worth it.

Kubbet Batata Helweh

Sweet Potato Kubbeh with Green Herby Salsa

Kubbeh is a dish that has many flavours, styles and techniques. It is most famous in Syria, where in one city alone they have over 20 different types of *kubbeh*.

Serves 8–10

1kg (2¼lb) sweet potatoes
600g (1lb 5oz) light coarse burghul (cracked wheat)
550–700ml (19–24fl oz) hot vegetable stock
1 teaspoon dried chilli flakes
1 tablespoon ground cumin
1 tablespoon ground coriander
2 tablespoons sea salt
1 large onion, diced
2 garlic cloves, crushed
2 tablespoons dried marjoram
a bunch of fresh flat-leaf parsley, chopped

For the salsa:

a bunch of fresh flat-leaf parsley
a small bunch of fresh coriander
1 red chilli
juice of 1 lemon
2 tablespoons white wine vinegar
4 tablespoons olive oil
1 tablespoon sea salt

For the filling:

150ml (5fl oz) olive oil, plus extra for frying
8 large onions, sliced
100g (3½oz) sumac
1 tablespoon sea salt
1 tablespoon black pepper

Preheat the oven to 200°C fan (220°C/425°F/Gas 7).

Roast the potatoes in their skins for about 30 minutes. You can cut them in half to make this process faster, which also helps to caramelize the potato, adding greater flavour. Drain the potatoes of any liquid and squeeze them to remove any excess juices.

Meanwhile, soak the burghul in the hot vegetable stock for about 5 minutes and then drain well.

Make the salsa while the potatoes are cooking. Chop all the ingredients and put them in a bowl, adding the lemon juice, vinegar and oil. Season with salt and set aside.

Peel the skins from the potatoes and mash them in a bowl. Add the mash to the drained burghul, then add all the spices and the salt, diced onion, garlic, marjoram and parsley. Mix well, taste and add more seasoning if needed.

To make the filling, heat the oil in a frying pan over a medium heat and sauté the onions until soft. Add the sumac, salt and pepper and set aside to cool.

Now to form your *kubbeh*. Take a golf ball-sized piece of the potato mix and roll into a ball. Use the thumb on your right hand to start hollowing the ball out, then insert a small amount of filling and mould the potato mix around the filling to seal. You should have an oval, rugby-ball shape. Repeat until all the mixture has been used.

Heat enough oil in a pan for shallow frying and fry the *kubbeh* for about 2–5 minutes until browned. Serve with the salsa and enjoy the sweetness of the spiced sweet potato with the tangy green salsa and sour sumac onions.

Tips: Instead of frying, you can also oven bake the *kubbeh* in a 200°C fan (220°C/425°F/Gas 7) oven for 30 minutes.

There are three different types of burghul (cracked wheat, see page 17). One is light coarse burghul as we use here; another is very fine, like semolina, and called light fine burghul (you definitely don't want to use that type here); and lastly, there is a dark coarse variety. Be sure to use the right one for this dish, otherwise the *kubbeh* will be too stodgy and won't hold their shape.

Vibrant Vegetarian

One of the many things that can be said about Palestinian food is that it offers a huge
and varied selection of vegetarian dishes, which are full of flavours that will exceed your
imagination. The colours and textures are so wonderful you could go for days eating just
vegetable dishes without even missing fish or meat. There are some that are simply a side dish
and others that carry a dinner on their own merit. In this chapter you will fall in love with
tangy paprika *hindbeh* (dandelion leaves), tabbouleh-stuffed vine leaves, oven-baked okra and
my grandmother's delicious *mussaka'a* (a spicy aubergine and tomato stew). The list is endless.

Hindbeh
Dandelion Leaves with Caramelized Onions & Sumac

During early spring in Palestine, especially near to Jericho (thought to be one of the most continually inhabited cities on earth), you will begin to notice some green grass-like plants growing along the mountainsides, in the cracks on the pavement and in some small gardens. Palestinians have been eating these plants for centuries as an integral part of their diet. One of these plants is called *hindbeh* (dandelion leaf). It is ever so popular and, on most occasions, not necessary to buy as you can just pick it from the wild. Dandelions are packed full of flavour and are a superfood, rich in antioxidants, protein, vitamins, iron and calcium. The list goes on but these little road-side plants have a lot to offer. You will find that the leaves are a little bitter, so it's best to soak them for about 10 minutes in water with a squeeze of lemon before using. If you don't want to forage, look for them in your local farmer's market.

Serves 4

200g (7oz) *hindbeh*
(dandelion leaves)
juice of 1 lemon
200ml (7fl oz) light olive oil,
plus extra for drizzling
4 large onions, cut in half
and sliced
2 teaspoons sea salt, plus
extra for seasoning
2 teaspoons sumac
1 teaspoon sweet paprika
1 pomegranate, seeded
flat bread, to serve

Put the dandelion leaves in a bowl of water with the juice of half a lemon, leaving the lemon in the water, and leave to soak for 10 minutes.

Heat the olive oil in a frying pan over a high heat. Make sure it is nice and hot before adding the onions. Cook for about 8–10 minutes, until they are lightly coloured.

Meanwhile, remove the dandelion leaves from the water and chop them into bite-sized pieces. Place them in a pot of salted boiling water (I add about 2 teaspoons salt) and boil for about 4 minutes. Drain and rinse under cold water to retain the fresh green colour, then drain again.

Add the dandelion leaves, sumac and sweet paprika to the onions, stir quickly, then set aside to cool down.

Tip the dandelion leaves mixture out onto a serving plate, drizzle with the remaining lemon juice and season with a little salt. Top with the pomegranate seeds and a final drizzle of olive oil. Serve with flat bread.

Tip: You can use kale if you can't find dandelion leaves – it tastes just as good and has the same healthy goodness. You can omit the soaking stage in the recipe above if you choose to use kale.

Bamyeh Bil Zeit
Oven-baked Okra with Olive Oil, Tomatoes & Onions

This is a one-pot wonder that has so many delicious components that burst with flavour in your mouth. I always feel like such an accomplished cook when I take this out of the oven and serve it to my friends or family and I am always amazed that such a delicious dish can come from just 5 minutes of preparation with very little messing about. The okra manages to hold its shape despite being cooked for a long time as you do not move it at all during the cooking process. It is covered with foil and left to cook in its own juices which results in a tangy, tart flavour matched with the smoothness of the okra and plenty of character from the garlic, chilli and coriander.

Serves 4–6

700g (1½lb) okra, tops cut off

4 onions, cut in half and
    sliced

4 tomatoes, cut in half and
    sliced

10 garlic cloves, sliced
    lengthways

1 tablespoon tomato purée

juice of 6 lemons

150ml (5fl oz) olive oil

1 teaspoon paprika

1 green chilli, chopped

2 tablespoons ground
    coriander

2–3 teaspoons sea salt

500ml (18fl oz) water

a bunch of fresh coriander

Preheat the oven to 190°C fan (210°C/415°F/Gas 6–7).

Place all the ingredients, except the water and half the fresh coriander, in a baking tray and mix together. Cover with the water and then cover the whole tray with foil.

Bake for about 60–75 minutes until you have a rich stew consistency. The liquid in the tray will become thick and sticky with the tomatoes and lemon, so keep checking the consistency during the cooking time. If at any time during the early stages of cooking the water has evaporated too much, simply add more.

Serve with fresh coriander scattered over the top and some bread, if liked.

Tip: Top the finished dish with some more chopped chilli for an added kick.

Fasoulia Bil Zeit
Green Beans with Spicy Tomato & Olive Oil Sauce

A varied meal with plenty of choice is the greatest gift to have and to give. Growing up, we used to enjoy this dish as an accompaniment to many meals as it is not overpowering but can still hold its own if you eat it by itself. *Fasoulia* is made with different beans in different parts of the Middle East. In Lebanon, for instance, they use butter beans, Egypt uses runner beans, but in Palestine, green beans are used. You can substitute them for other beans if you wish, just bear in mind that cooking times may vary. We use lots of chilli as this is a very commonly eaten dish in Gaza, which is famous for chilli as it is on the spice route to the Mediterranean. The quick cooking time is another bonus; the dish is healthy and full of goodness because it's not been through a long cooking process. I usually eat this with toasted flat bread but it is just as satisfying on its own.

Serves 4

5 tablespoons olive oil, plus extra for drizzling

2 large onions, chopped

1–2 heads of garlic, peeled and chopped

1 large red chilli, sliced

300g (10½oz) green beans, ends trimmed

250ml (8½fl oz) tomato passata

sea salt

Heat the oil in a heavy-based saucepan. Add the chopped onions and let them sauté slightly until soft and translucent, but not brown.

Once they have softened, add the garlic and let them sweat. You want the flavour to come out of these two ingredients as they will hold the dish together. Add 1 teaspoon salt to release more flavour.

Add the chilli and green beans. Cook until the beans are cooked to your liking – I usually leave it for about 5–7 minutes and then add the tomato passata. When you add the tomato, it will stop the cooking process of the beans and will take much longer due to the acidity, but it also helps to keep the beans green.

Check for seasoning and add more salt and chilli if needed. Continue to simmer for 5 minutes. Leave on the hob until you are ready to eat, and then drizzle with extra oil before serving. This should be a really oniony and garlicky dish with a kick of chilli.

Yalanji
Tabbouleh-stuffed Vine Leaves

If I was going to live only one more day on this beautiful earth, this would be one of my last meal requests. I don't know what it is that makes me absolutely fall in love with this every time I eat it, but it has my heart. The tartness, the stickiness of the rice, the flavours, the slow cooking . . . all of it just gets me excited. It is a little time consuming to prepare, but I assure you, with a little practice you'll get quicker. This is also one of my elder sister, Lara's, favourite dishes. She loves vine leaves – especially the tangy lemon ones at the bottom of the pot. It reminds her of parties when we were younger as it was always a staple dish.

Serves 8

680ml (1lb 7oz) jar of
   vine leaves in brine (or
   400g/14oz fresh ones)
500g (1lb 2oz) Egyptian rice
   (or pudding rice)
1 large onion, diced
a bunch of spring onions,
   sliced
a large bunch of fresh
   flat-leaf parsley, chopped
7 tomatoes, 3 chopped and
   4 sliced into rings
350ml (12fl oz) tomato
   passata
4 tablespoons olive oil,
   plus extra for drizzling
2 teaspoons sea salt
juice of 1 lemon, plus extra
   for drizzling
1 green chilli

Boil the vine leaves in water for 6–8 minutes to soften them and rinse away the salt. Drain, separate the leaves and place them on kitchen paper to drain any excess water away.

Put the rice, onions, spring onions, parsley and chopped tomatoes in a bowl and mix together. Stir in the passata, add the olive oil and season with salt. Add the lemon juice and mix everything together. It should taste like tabbouleh with rice – tangy and delicious. Set aside.

Put one of the vine leaves on a clean surface in front of you, dull side up (the slightly shinier side should be facing down). Put a teaspoon of the rice stuffing on the lower part of the vine leaf near the stem and then fold the bottom edge up to just cover the stuffing. Bring in the sides and then continue to roll upwards (see page 129). Repeat until you have stuffed all of the vine leaves.

Arrange the sliced tomatoes over the bottom of a heavy-based saucepan to protect the leaves as they cook. Arrange the stuffed leaves in a circle around the base, creating height but making sure they are all tightly compressed so that they stay together during cooking. This is very important as if they have too much room to move, they will open up and fall apart during cooking.

Top with the chilli, then cover with enough water to reach just to the top of the vine leaves. Place a plate, face down, over the vine leaves to secure them and then simmer over a medium-low heat for 2 hours until the water has evaporated and the rice is cooked. If after that time, the water hasn't evaporated, but they are cooked, just carefully drain the excess water away.

Squeeze some lemon juice over the vine leaves and drizzle with olive oil while they are still warm, then leave them to rest for about 15 minutes. When you are ready to serve, remove the plate, place your serving tray over the pan, say a little prayer and flip! The vine leaves are best eaten warm, but are still delicious enjoyed the next day.

Tip: Use any leftover rice stuffing to stuff an aubergine or courgette and add it to the pan with the leaves or keep it in the freezer for next time.

Sabanekh Wa Ruz Bil Sha'riyeh

Spinach Stew with Vermicelli Rice

As a child I often suffered from an iron deficiency and my mum would cook food full of iron to make me feel better. She always had a great understanding of different foods and how good they are for you even before it was fashionable to have such knowledge. So livers and all things green were on the menu for me, and this spinach and rice dish was the one I loved the most for its sour, spicy and salty flavour. Many of the rice-based dishes in this book are made with this Egyptian rice (a short-grain variety), cooked with vermicelli.

Serves 4

4 tablespoons vegetable oil

1 large onion, chopped

1 whole head of garlic, chopped

750g (1lb 10oz) fresh baby leaf spinach

1 vegetable stock cube (optional)

500ml (18fl oz) water

1 green chilli, cut lengthways

juice of 1 lemon

sea salt

For the vermicelli rice:

2 tablespoons vegetable oil

4 vermicelli nests, crushed

350g (12oz) Egyptian rice (or pudding or basmati)

625ml (22fl oz) water

2 teaspoons sea salt

Heat the oil in a saucepan over a medium heat. Sauté the onions for 5 minutes until softened and then add the garlic and cook for another 5–8 minutes.

Add the spinach and move it around in the pan until it begins to wilt – it will look like it's not going to wilt, but have faith, it will.

Once the spinach has wilted, add the stock cube and water and a little salt and mix to make sure the stock cube has dissolved. Add the chilli and cook for 10 minutes.

To make the rice, heat the oil in another saucepan and toast the crushed vermicelli. Once it has browned slightly, add the rice and toss it around the pan to even it out. Cover with the water and season with salt. Cook over a medium heat for 20 minutes.

Serve the rice with the spinach stew and squeeze some lemon juice all over.

Tips: If you are cooking for meat eaters, you can use a chicken stock cube instead of the vegetable one to give it a fuller-bodied flavour.

I like to eat this with radishes and spring onions, too.

Sabanekh Wa Jibneh
Spinach & Cheese Parcels

These delicious parcels are served all over the Middle East. My mother and sisters were the best at making them in our family. I love eating them and make them in batches for the freezer as they keep so well. They remind me of home and my family and all my aunties sitting together folding and wrapping them, talking and laughing and not even concentrating on what they were doing, but always producing the best results. This is such a good meal as it has so much flavour packed into such a small package. It is easy to make ahead of time, nice eaten hot, warm or cold, and is perfect for baking when friends come round.

Serves 6–8

250g (9oz) spinach, washed and dried

a bunch of fresh dill, chopped

a bunch of fresh chives, chopped

a bunch of fresh flat-leaf parsley, chopped

500g (1lb 2oz) feta cheese, crumbled

2 eggs, beaten

1 teaspoon ground nutmeg

1 x 400g (14oz) chilled packet of filo pastry

150g (5½oz) butter, melted

sea salt and black pepper

Preheat the oven to 220°C fan (240°C/465°F/Gas 9).

Put the spinach and herbs in a large bowl. Add the feta, egg, nutmeg and seasoning and mix well. Set aside while you prepare the filo pastry.

Take 3 sheets of filo at a time, brush each with melted butter and then layer them together, with the short edge closest to you. Place a handful of filling along the short edge, and begin rolling the pastry upwards. Tuck the corners in to secure the roll and continue rolling until you get to the end.

Carefully twist the roll into a snail shape – they have a tendency to break because filo is like paper, so move slowly. Repeat with all the filo and filling and place each roll in a non-stick baking tin or tray (or line a tin or tray with baking parchment). Brush the rolls with melted butter.

Bake for about 20–25 minutes or until they have turned golden brown. Remove from the oven and serve warm.

Tip: If you don't want to roll these parcels into a snail shape, you can simply layer the pastry and filling to make a raised tart and bake in a deep baking tray.

Batata Harra
Spicy Coriander & Garlic Potatoes

Batata Harra is literally translated as 'spicy potatoes'. I love, love, love this dish and don't make it nearly often enough. It is usually made with just potatoes, but I like to use sweet potatoes too, to add a little colour and sweetness to the spicy aftertaste. This is a traditional accompaniment in Middle Eastern cuisine and is served in most restaurants – although I find restaurant versions too oily. My homemade version is much better (and my dad's is pretty good, too) as I add more of everything I like. It is one of those dishes that is a little naughty, but very, very nice.

Serves 4

175ml (6fl oz) olive oil
3 potatoes, peeled and
    diced
1 large sweet potato, diced
    (optional)
1 teaspoon cayenne pepper
5 garlic cloves, crushed
1 small red chilli, chopped
2–3 tablespoons sea salt
juice of 2–3 lemons
a small bunch of fresh
    coriander, chopped
Tabasco sauce and
    Khubez (pita bread,
    see page 48), to serve

Preheat the oven to 190°C fan (210°C/415°F/Gas 6–7).

Coat the base of a baking tray with the olive oil and place it in the oven to heat for 10 minutes.

Add the potatoes, season with the cayenne, garlic, chilli and salt and toss together so the potatoes are well coated. Bake in the oven for 40 minutes, tossing them every now and then while they cook.

When the potatoes are crispy and golden, stir through some lemon juice and the coriander. Serve with Tabasco and bread to soak up all the juices.

Teta Huda's Mussaka'a
Fried & Baked Spicy Aubergine & Tomato Stew

Mussaka'a is one of my family's all-time favourites. It is easy, delicious and packed full of flavour with just a few ingredients. My mother makes this for my father a lot at the request of Teta Huda, his mother – if there is a dish to remember someone by, this would be his dish. He never used to eat aubergines, and in fact hated them, until he met my mother, but through her cooking she converted him. Making this ahead of time is great as it is best served cold or at room temperature (*mussaka'a* literally means 'cold'). This recipe is for my dad. I have used the recipe from my grandmother Huda, who never stopped persevering in her aubergine mission with my father!

Serves 4

400ml (14fl oz) sunflower oil

2 large aubergines, chopped into 2.5cm (1 inch) cubes

4–6 tablespoons olive oil

1 whole head of garlic, peeled and cut into thick slivers

1 large onion, chopped

2 hot green chillies, halved lengthways

250g (9oz) Datterini tomatoes (see note), halved

500ml (18fl oz) tomato passata

sea salt and black pepper

Preheat the oven to 200°C fan (220°C/425°F/Gas 7).

Heat the sunflower oil in a large saucepan over a high heat until it is very hot, then add the aubergines. Lightly fry for about 5–10 minutes (depending on the size of your chunks), then remove from the heat, sprinkle with salt and set aside.

Heat the olive oil in a large saucepan over a medium heat and fry the garlic and onions until they begin to gently caramelize. Add the chillies and fry a little to release the intensity of the flavour. Add the tomatoes and cook until they split open and cook down in the pan with the garlic, onions and chilli.

Once they have reduced slightly, add the passata and leave it to simmer gently for about 10 minutes – you are looking for a deep, rich garlic flavour with a spicy kick. Season to taste.

Once it has reduced by about one-third, add the fried aubergines and mix together. Transfer everything to an ovenproof dish and bake for about 30–35 minutes until the liquid has reduced by about one-third again as you don't want a really saucy dish – it should be thick but with some movement.

Remove from the oven, taste to check the seasoning and adjust if needed and then leave it to cool. Transfer to the fridge to chill. This dish should be eaten cold or at room temperature. Enjoy with warm toasted *Khubez* (pita bread, see page 48).

Tip: Datterini tomatoes are my preferred type of tomato to use in cooking – they are far juicier and plumper than other varieties and really taste as a tomato should.

Mama's Mutabbal
Smoky Aubergine Dip – Mama's Way

I think this has to be one of the most moreish dishes I know. It is salty, smoky and sweet with tang and citrus, and not forgetting the chilli kick at the end. I love making this the way my mum makes it. It is much lighter than the versions you would have in a restaurant. This is the most delicious way to eat aubergine, when it is smoked and bursting at the seams in the oven, or if you are lucky, on a gas hob. I love watching the skin splinter and burst and can literally taste the smokiness simply by the way it looks. This is a regular feature at our dinner table and is always served without fail at barbecues.

Serves 4–6

2 large aubergines
2 tablespoons sea salt,
  plus extra for seasoning
olive oil, for drizzling
2 tablespoons tahini
  (see page 21)
4 tablespoons Greek yogurt
juice of 2 lemons
1 garlic clove
1 green chilli, chopped
pomegranate seeds,
  to serve

Begin by searing the aubergines. Drizzle them with salt and olive oil and either cook in an oven preheated to its highest setting until they are charred (about 30 minutes); or hold over a gas flame until you see the skin scorch all over – this way is quite quick, so use your judgement and take care. It is important to scorch the aubergine from the outside to get the smoky flavour.

Once the aubergines are soft and browned, open the skin, scoop out the flesh and chop into smaller pieces. Put it in a sieve and set aside for about 5 minutes to drain the excess water away.

Put the chopped aubergine in a bowl and add the tahini, yogurt, lemon juice, garlic and salt. Mix it all together and taste to see if you need any more salt or yogurt – it is really down to personal taste.

Add the chilli and mix through – I usually add it at the end as I don't like it to overpower the dish.

Drizzle with some olive oil and top with pomegranate seeds to serve. I usually eat this with the *Kubbeh Bil Sanniyeh* (see page 78).

Pumpkin Mutabbal

This pumpkin *mutabbal* is a very popular dish from my auntie Nuha who lives in Amman in Jordan. She is very well known for her cooking and will be so proud that this recipe is in the book.

Serves 6-8

1 large pumpkin

1 whole head of garlic, cloves separated, skin on

a bunch of fresh thyme

olive oil, to drizzle

4 tablespoons Greek yogurt

3 tablespoons tahini (see page 21)

juice of 4 lemons

1 pomegranate, seeded

a small bunch of fresh mint, to serve

sea salt, to taste

Preheat the oven to 190°C fan (210°C/415°F/Gas 6–7). Cut the pumpkin into crescents, removing the seeds, and place in a baking tray. Add the garlic, salt and thyme and drizzle generously with olive oil. Roast for 45 minutes until golden. Leave the pumpkin to cool, before removing the skins and draining them of any excess water.

Transfer the pumpkin to a food processor or blender and squeeze in the garlic cloves from their skins. Blitz, then add the yogurt, tahini, lemon juice and some salt. Mix well, then season with more salt to taste. Transfer to the fridge for at least 2 hours, or overnight, to thicken.

Top with pomegranate seeds and mint and serve with warm *Khubez* (pita bread, see page 48). Make big batches of this. It can keep for almost a week.

Tip: Squash and sweet potato can be used instead of pumpkin if preferred.

Chunky Mutabbal

This is a more rustic version of the traditional *mutabbal* (see opposite). The combination of these flavours is like a burst of colour in your mouth.

Serves 4

4 large aubergines, cut into chunks

1 whole head of garlic

150–200ml (5–7fl oz) olive oil, plus extra to drizzle

juice of 2 lemons

1 red chilli, halved and sliced

a bunch of fresh parsley, chopped roughly

1–2 pomegranates, seeded

sea salt and black pepper

Preheat the oven to 220°C fan (240°C/465°F/Gas 9). Put the aubergines on a non-stick baking tray and break the garlic cloves on top, keeping them in their skins. Drizzle all over with olive oil, season with salt and a little pepper and toss together.

Bake in the oven for about 30 minutes – you want them to colour slightly and crisp up. Bake for another 15 minutes for an extra chargrilled effect.

Once they are ready, squeeze the lemon juice on top and add the chilli and parsley. Add a little more salt and olive oil if you wish. Scatter with pomegranate seeds – this will make it almost jewel-like and really add a citrus punch and beautiful ruby colour to the dish. Serve and enjoy.

Khudar Mehshi
Stuffed Vegetables

Stuffed aubergines, peppers, tomatoes and potatoes make such an easy, healthy and cost-effective meal, while being hearty and delicious at the same time. Who knew that such simple ingredients could create such a wonderful dish that is so moreish and ridiculously tasty? This is food that can be made in advance for sit-down meals or packed for lunches, picnics or buffets. It is a great vegetarian option – I'm not even a vegetarian, but this is at the top of my list of favourites. It is best served at room temperature to let all the flavours settle and soak in. I ate this dish for about three days straight when I first made it as I made so much, and I have to say it tasted better and better each day I ate it.

Serves 4–6

2 potatoes

2 beef tomatoes

2 aubergines

2 peppers (assorted colours)

300g (10½oz) Egyptian rice
  (or pudding rice)

700ml (1¼ pints) tomato
  passata

1 large onion, finely
  chopped

1 large courgette, cut into
  cubes

a bunch of fresh chives,
  chopped

6 tablespoons olive oil

a large bunch of fresh
  flat-leaf parsley, chopped

350ml (12fl oz) water

sea salt and black pepper

Preheat the oven to 180°C fan (200°C/400°F/Gas 6).

Peel and core the potatoes. Slice the tops off the tomatoes, aubergines and peppers, hollow out and set aside. Keep the tops of the tomatoes and peppers to create lids.

Roughly chop the flesh from one of the aubergines and put in a bowl. Add the rice, half the passata, the onion, courgettes, chives, 4 tablespoons of the olive oil and three-quarters of the parsley. Season and mix well.

Fill the vegetables with the mixture but don't overfill as the rice won't cook. Put the tops back on where needed and place the stuffed vegetables in an ovenproof dish that will fit them snugly.

Add the water and the remaining olive oil to the rest of the passata, season with salt and pepper and pour the mixture over and around the vegetables.

Bake for 1½ hours, turning the vegetables halfway through and just before serving. The vegetables should be soft, browned and almost falling apart. Sprinkle with the remaining parsley and serve.

Sandweeshet Betinjan Wa Arnabeet
Spicy Fried Aubergine & Cauliflower Sandwiches

When my siblings and I were younger, my mother would whip up these sandwiches for us. We would take them to school for lunch, which would be so different to anything the other children were eating. I have mentioned before that my father didn't like aubergines until he met my mother. Through her love of food, she transformed his feelings towards them and he began asking for them – especially these little parcels of joy. I often make this when I'm feeling lazy and want a taste of home.

Serves 4

400ml (14fl oz) sunflower oil

2 aubergines, sliced into rings

1 head of cauliflower, cut into florets

2 teaspoons sea salt

4 wraps or *Khubez* (pita bread, see page 48)

juice of 1 lemon

Tabasco sauce, to serve

Put the oil in a pan and bring it up to a high heat. Put several pieces of aubergine in the pan and cook for about 3–5 minutes, then add some of the cauliflower and cook for another 2–5 minutes until they turn a caramel colour. Transfer the cooked vegetables to a baking tray and season with salt. Cook the rest of the aubergine and cauliflower in batches and add them to the tray.

Once cooked, fill each wrap or pita with the cooked vegetables, squeeze over some lemon juice, drizzle with Tabasco, fold and eat.

Tip: You can also add some sliced red chilli and rocket, if liked.

Halloumi Meshwi
Pan-grilled Halloumi with Lemon

This dish evokes memories of sandy beaches and holidays for me. It is light, tangy, creamy and so good you just won't be able to stop eating it. You can use any non melting cheese like *akkawi*, but I prefer to cook this the traditional way with halloumi. I often make this as a snack when I'm feeling a bit peckish.

Serves 4

2 tablespoons plain flour

1 teaspoon dried chilli flakes

2 x 200g (7oz) packs of halloumi, cut lengthways into 1.5cm (½ inch) slices

3–4 tablespoons vegetable oil

juice of 1 lemon or lime

black pepper

In a shallow bowl, season the flour with the chilli flakes and some pepper. Dip the halloumi pieces in the flour and turn to coat.

Heat the oil in a pan over a medium heat and shallow fry the halloumi for about 1–2 minutes. Once it has begun to brown, turn the pieces over and cook the other side for another 1–2 minutes.

When ready, plate up the golden halloumi and squeeze over some lemon or lime juice. Eat straightaway otherwise it will get chewy.

Burghul Wa Kousa
Burghul (Cracked Wheat) with Courgettes & Tomato Sauce

My mother's family are originally from Safad, and in this area and the surrounding mountainous areas, burghul (cracked wheat) is eaten regularly to bulk up dishes and create hearty meals. I have made this for so many people and always wonder what they are going to make of it as it is so simple, but the comments are always positive. I adore this dish and make it most weeks as I love the dark coarse burghul with its fabulous texture and nutty aroma.

Serves 6

50ml (2fl oz) olive oil, plus an
    extra 3 tablespoons
    for drizzling
1 large onion, chopped, plus
    1 onion, quartered, to serve
2 teaspoons sea salt
1 teaspoon black pepper
3–4 tablespoons tomato
    purée
juice of ½ lemon
4 courgettes, cut into 1.5cm
    (½ inch) slices and then
    into quarters
400g (14oz) dark coarse
    burghul (cracked wheat)
a bunch of fresh mint
a bunch of spring onions

Heat the olive oil (reserving the 3 tablespoons until later) in a saucepan over a high heat and sauté the chopped onion for about 5 minutes. Add the salt, pepper, tomato purée and lemon juice and mix.

Add the courgettes and mix well. Add the burghul (cracked wheat) and enough water to just cover the mixture – don't add too much as the burghul will expand and become too soggy.

Cook over a medium to high heat for about 5–6 minutes, then turn the heat down to low and cook for 10–12 minutes until the water has evaporated.

Mix the burghul with a fork and drizzle with the reserved olive oil. Garnish with the mint, spring onions and quartered onions and serve with bread and yogurt, if liked. I love to eat every bite of the burghul with some onions, mint and yogurt to get the very best flavour.

Salatet Fattoush
Traditional Chopped Salad with Toasted Bread

Fattoush is a Levantine bread salad made from toasted or fried pieces of pita bread combined with mixed greens and other vegetables; it is one of the most commonly eaten salads in the Middle East. The most important part of this dish is the toasted bread, which sets it apart from other salads. My family eat this every day during Ramadan and it's one of my mother's favourites. Who knew a little toasted bread could improve a salad so much? So very easy to do and so delicious.

Serves 6

3 small *Khubez* (pita bread, see page 48), cut into diamond shapes
1 head of baby Gem lettuce
1 head of romaine lettuce
1 tomato
1 cucumber
½ green pepper
½ red pepper
100g (3½) radishes
a small bunch of fresh mint, chopped
5 tablespoons olive oil
1 teaspoon sea salt
2 tablespoons red wine vinegar
1 teaspoon sumac
juice of 1 lemon
3 teaspoons za'atar (see page 17)
1 pomegranate, seeded

Preheat the oven to 180°C fan (200°C/400°F/Gas 6).

Put the pita pieces on a baking tray and bake for 5–8 minutes until lightly golden brown.

Cut the lettuce and all the vegetables into small, even-sized pieces and mix them together. Add the mint leaves and mix these through the salad.

Mix the olive oil, salt, vinegar, sumac, lemon juice and za'atar together and pour the dressing over the salad. Add the toasted bread and sprinkle the pomegranate seeds all over the top before serving.

Fennel, Apple & Pomegranate Salad

When I had my restaurant, Baity Kitchen, this salad was served all through the year. It was so popular and still is – I always make it for parties, supper clubs and events. The sweetness of the crisp apple against the aniseed flavour of the fennel works so well in this popular salad from Gaza. A real gem of a salad, literally, with all the jewel-like seeds of the pomegranate sprinkled through.

Serves 4

2 fennel bulbs, sliced into half
  moons
4 Pink Lady apples, sliced
  into half moons
1 lemon, for squeezing
1 pomegranate, seeded
a bunch of fresh dill, roughly
  chopped

For the dressing:
200ml (7fl oz) olive oil
75ml (2¾fl oz) apple cider
  vinegar
2 tablespoons caster sugar
1 teaspoon sea salt

Put the fennel and apple in a bowl and squeeze over the lemon juice. Turn them in the juice to prevent them going brown.

Add the pomegranate seeds and dill and mix together well.

Mix the dressing ingredients together in a small bowl or jar. Pour it over the salad and toss so that it is well combined.

Tip: Adding some cooked basmati rice to this salad makes a nice change sometimes. It is such a delicious way to enjoy any leftovers as the rice will soak up all the tangy sauce. Only add room temperature or cold rice, otherwise the heat will make the salad limp.

Salatet Banadora Wa Bassal
Tomato & Parsley Salad with Red Onions

This salad evokes a sense of home and fresh produce – I have it most days and serve it at my supper clubs.

Serves 4

4 large plum tomatoes, cut
  into wedges
a bunch of fresh flat-leaf
  parsley, chopped
1 small red onion, cut in half
  and sliced
juice of ½ lemon
2–4 tablespoons olive oil
sea salt

Mix the tomatoes, parsley and onions together in a bowl. Mix in the lemon juice and olive oil and sprinkle with salt.

Enjoy this simple, classic side dish.

Salateť Il Rahib
Monk's Aubergine Salad

This salad is originally from Lebanon. It is thought to be named after a monk who created this dish from the produce he tended in his garden. It is a delicious staple on our table that is punchy and full of gorgeously tangy and crunchy vegetables, and of course the smoky aubergine that is complemented by all the other ingredients. It is one of my personal favourites that I have been cooking for years and years. Thanks go to my mum and my aunties for teaching me how to make it.

Serves 4–6

2 large aubergines

150ml (5fl oz) olive oil, plus extra for rubbing

½ red pepper, deseeded and chopped

½ green pepper, deseeded and chopped

1 plum tomato, chopped

½ onion, chopped

3 spring onions, chopped

a small bunch of fresh flat-leaf parsley, chopped

1 small garlic clove, crushed

1 heaped teaspoon dried mint

juice of 1–2 lemons

1 pomegranate, seeded

sea salt

toasted *Khubez* (pita bread, see page 48), to serve

Preheat the oven to 200°C fan (220°C/425°F/Gas 7) and line a baking tray with baking parchment.

Use a sharp knife to pierce the aubergines on all sides and rub them with some oil. Place the aubergines on the prepared baking tray. Bake for about 35–40 minutes, until they are charred and brown (don't worry too much about burning them as you want that smoky effect).

Meanwhile, begin to prepare the rest of the salad. Mix the peppers, tomato, onion and spring onions in a bowl. Add the parsley, garlic and dried mint and mix together.

Squeeze in the lemon juice and add some salt to taste (about 1–2 teaspoons) and the olive oil.

When the aubergines are ready, take them out of the oven and leave them until they are cool enough to handle. Cut them in half and scoop out the flesh, discarding the skin. Roughly chop the flesh and add it to the salad.

Mix everything together, taste to check the seasoning and add more oil, salt or lemon juice if needed. Top with the pomegranate seeds and serve with *Khubez* (pita bread).

Salatet Arnabeet Ma' Tahineh Wa Bassal
Cauliflower Salad with Tahini & Onions

Cauliflower has gained a good reputation as a healthy ingredient recently due to its high levels of vitamins C, K, B2, B1, B6 and fatty acids. This beauty is eaten everywhere in Palestine and has been for thousands of years. My favourite cauliflower recipes are this one and the Spicy Fried Aubergine and Cauliflower Sandwich on page 107. Here is a super simple and quick recipe that I used to make in my restaurant, Baity Kitchen. It will most certainly be a head turner for those who normally shy away from such vegetables.

Serves 4

2 heads of cauliflower, broken into florets
3 tablespoons olive oil
1 large red onion, sliced into half moons
2 teaspoons za'atar (see page 17)
a small bunch of rocket
150g (5½oz) large green olives (preferably Middle Eastern)
2 tomatoes, cut into wedges
1 red chilli, sliced into rings
sea salt

For the dressing:

4 tablespoons tahini (see page 21)
2 tablespoons Greek yogurt
juice of 4 lemons
2 teaspoons sea salt

Preheat the oven to 200°C fan (220°C/425°C/Gas 7). Put the cauliflower florets on a baking tray. Pour over the oil and scatter over half the onions, the za'atar and a sprinkle of salt and mix so that it is all coated. Bake for about 20–25 minutes.

When the cauliflower has cooked and charred, remove the tray from the oven and add the rocket, olives, tomatoes and sliced chilli and mix together.

To make the dressing, mix the tahini, yogurt and lemon juice together in a small bowl. Add the salt and a little water if you need more liquid – you are aiming for the consistency of double cream. Once you have a nice tangy flavour that you are happy with, drizzle the dressing over the top of the cauliflower salad and serve warm.

Kabees Khudar
Pickled Vegetables

I love making everything by hand and from scratch and making pickles is particularly amazing. You can add whatever spices or herbs you like, mixed with any vegetable you like. My favourites are beetroot, carrots, cauliflower and cucumber. I use the same vinegar base for all my pickles, but change the flavouring to suit the vegetable. You can easily adapt these to your liking, and if you use bigger jars just add a bit more water and vinegar.

Makes 1 medium 500ml (18fl oz) mason jar

For the pickling mix:
150ml (5fl oz) white wine vinegar
350ml (12fl oz) water
1 teaspoon caster sugar

For pickled turnips:
3 turnips, peeled and cut into chunks
1 beetroot, peeled and cut into chunks
1 green chilli, sliced lengthways

For pickled cucumbers & chillies:
6 small cucumbers
½ teaspoon dried chilli flakes

For pickled cauliflower & carrots:
½ head of cauliflower, broken into small florets
1-2 carrots, sliced
1 teaspoon pink peppercorns
1 teaspoon chopped fresh dill
4-6 pieces of lemon rind

FOR PICKLED TURNIPS
Mix the pickling mix ingredients together in a large bowl until the sugar has dissolved. Put the turnips, beetroot and chilli in a clean, sterilized mason jar and pour the pickling mix over the top – make sure the turnips are completely submerged. Seal the jar and leave to marinate for at least 1 week. You want the beetroot colour to permeate the turnips and give them a fabulous deep pink colour. It will keep in the fridge for about 2–4 weeks.

FOR PICKLED CUCUMBERS & CHILLIES
Mix the pickling mix ingredients together in a large bowl until the sugar has dissolved. Stand the cucumbers upright inside a clean, sterilized mason jar, adding the chilli flakes as you go. Pour over the pickling mix and make sure the cucumbers are completely submerged. Seal the jar and leave to marinate for at least 1 week. It will keep in the fridge for about 2–4 weeks.

FOR PICKLED CAULIFLOWER & CARROTS
Mix the pickling mix ingredients together in a large bowl until the sugar has dissolved. Put the cauliflower and carrots in a clean, sterilized mason jar and mix in the peppercorns, dill and lemon rind. Pour the pickling mix over the top and make sure the vegetables are completely submerged. Seal the jar and leave to marinate for at least 1 week. It will keep in the fridge for about 2–4 weeks.

Tip: Use more water in your pickling mix if you are using a larger jar.

To sterilize jars: Wash the jars and lids in hot soapy water. Turn them upside down and place on a baking tray in an oven preheated to 160°C fan (180°C/350°F/Gas 4) for about 15 minutes. Remove the jars and fill with your choice of pickle or preserve. Try not to let any food touch the rim of the jar as it will create bacteria. Seal the jars and then put away until using.

The Mighty Lamb & Chicken

Palestine is a land of meat eaters (even if you were starting to think you had bought a vegetarian cookbook), with lamb and chicken being the most widely eaten. Lamb has a very distinct, identifiable flavour and we like our food to stand out, which is why it is used a lot, rather than beef or pork. You can substitute most dishes with beef if you prefer, it will not ruin the dish, so it's really just down to personal taste. Pork is never used, and pigs are not actually kept as farm animals in Palestine as it is mainly a Muslim country; I have personally never seen an authentic Middle Eastern dish with pork in it. Palestinian meat dishes are tender, fall-off-the-bone and succulent and are so varied in flavour that I am sure they will become firm favourites in your home in no time.

Makloubeh

'Upside-down' Spiced Rice with Lamb & Aubergines

Makloubeh is a traditional Palestinian dish that consists of meat, rice and fried vegetables placed in a pot, which is then flipped upside down when served – hence the name *makloubeh*, which translates literally as 'upside down'. We often make this dish for important events, such as Eid, Ramadan and family birthdays as it is a labour of love. The cinnamon in the rice really makes this dish stand out. It's absolutely worth the effort involved and a real showstopper. My whole family love this dish – we make it in many different ways, but this version is the one I like the most. I personally like adding potatoes to it but I have stuck to the way my mother makes it here. My niece Thalia absolutely adores it – she only eats it when my mother cooks it as she says it makes her tummy happy.

Serves 6–8

- 1kg (2¼lb) lamb shoulder, cubed
- 2 onions, quartered
- 450ml (15fl oz) vegetable oil
- 3 aubergines, peeled in stripes, leaving some skin intact, then sliced into 3cm (1¼ inch) rings (see page 136)
- 750g (1lb 10 oz) Egyptian rice (or pudding or basmati rice)
- 3 teaspoons ground cinnamon
- 2 teaspoons black pepper
- 3 teaspoons sea salt, plus extra for seasoning
- 2 tablespoons olive oil
- 2 large tomatoes, sliced
- 1 tablespoon chopped parsley
- 150g (5½oz) whole skinned, blanched and toasted almonds
- 150g (5½oz) thick Greek yogurt, to serve

Put the lamb and onions in a saucepan, cover with water without stirring and then bring to the boil. Reduce the heat and simmer for 1 hour, covered with a lid. Remove any scum that appears on the surface and keep doing this until no more scum appears. Once the meat is cooked, remove it from the water but keep the water in the pan.

Heat the vegetable oil in a separate pan and shallow fry the aubergine for 3 minutes on each side, then drain on kitchen paper and season with salt.

Tip the rice into a bowl, adding the cinnamon, pepper, salt and olive oil and mix well.

Arrange the tomatoes in the base of a deep pan. Scatter a handful of rice over the tomatoes and layer half the lamb on top, followed by half the aubergine, then top with rice. Repeat these layers, finishing with a layer of rice.

Cover with the reserved lamb cooking water to about 3cm (1¼ inch) over the top (add a little more water if you don't have enough) and cover with a lid. Simmer over a medium-low heat for 30–40 minutes without stirring at all – once cooked, you want to be able to tip the dish out in one piece, like a cake.

Leave to cool slightly, then place an upturned plate larger than the mouth of your pan on top and carefully turn everything over to flip the *makloubeh* onto the plate. Sprinkle with the parsley and toasted nuts and serve with yogurt.

Kufta Bil Tahineh
Minced Lamb Kufta with Tangy Tahini Sauce

The flavour of the sharp tahini sauce with the beautiful spiced lamb mince in this dish is such a wonderful contrast in your mouth – it's like an ivory velvet snow covering rough mountains of goodness. I love tahini. It goes so well with meat and fish and is also great in salad dressings. It adds another dimension to this recipe and the sharpness of the lemon juice makes the whole thing divine.

This recipe is so simple that you really can't go wrong, and the end result actually looks like you have put a lot of effort into making something that tastes so great. That's the wonder of cooking – there are so many ingredients that marry well, that you can just keep making new things all the time with similar ingredients in different combinations. This dish will have you dreaming of the next time you will make it. Or hoping that no one else will want the last slice . . .

Serves 4–6

900g (1lb 15oz) lamb mince
1 onion, chopped
a bunch of fresh flat-leaf
  parsley, chopped
2–3 teaspoons sea salt
8 tablespoons tahini
  (see page 21)
3 tablespoons Greek yogurt
juice of 4 lemons
120ml (4fl oz) water
black pepper

Preheat the oven to 200°C fan (220°C/425°F/Gas 7).

Mix the lamb mince with the onion and parsley and add about 2 teaspoons of the salt and a little pepper. Tip it into an ovenproof tray or dish and gently pat the mixture down, making indents every 2cm (¾ inch) to create little dips in the surface. Do not press the meat down too tightly though as you don't want to have a dense texture.

Mix the tahini and yogurt together and add the lemon juice. It will begin to seize and thicken but don't worry, it will loosen up. Add the water and check for taste, adding a little salt if needed. You want it to be zingy and a little runny. Set aside.

Bake the meat for about 15 minutes, until browned, then take the tray out of the oven. Pour the tahini mix all over the surface. Return the tray to the oven for another 10–15 minutes, or until slightly charred on top.

Serve with green peppers, chilli, radishes and some *Khubez* (pita bread, see page 48).

Tip: Transform the above dish into *Kufta Bil Batata Wa Banadora* – a very similar dish using vegetables as a topping. My mum would make these side by side so we could have both as some of us liked one more than the other. Prepare the mince, onion and parsley and press into an ovenproof tray as above. Layer 2 peeled and thinly sliced large potatoes and 4–6 thinly sliced large tomatoes on top of the *kufta*, overlapping as you go, and keep going until you have covered the surface completely. Bake for about 30 minutes, checking it every now and again to make sure the potatoes are cooking. Serve as above.

Kousa Bil Laban

Middle Eastern Courgettes stuffed with Lamb

Kousa Bil Laban is a wonderful marriage of just a few ingredients that combine to create something simply delicious. This dish will strike a chord with most Palestinians and Arabs as it is something that will have been served at everyone's table over and over again. I am not sure where this actually originated but it has been in our family for generations and it is bound to become a staple in your family once you've tasted it.

Serves 4–6

4 tablespoons olive oil

500g (1lb 2oz) lean lamb mince

1½ onions, chopped

2 teaspoons sea salt

1 teaspoon black pepper

2 teaspoons ground cinnamon

15 courgettes (preferably Middle Eastern)

4 tablespoons sunflower oil

1kg (2¼lb) Greek yogurt

1 egg

2 tablespoons cornflour

Vermicelli Rice (see page 93), to serve

Put the olive oil in a pan over a high heat and fry the lamb and onions for about 7–8 minutes until the onions are softened and slightly browned and the lamb cooked through. Add the salt, pepper and cinnamon and mix through. Check for seasoning and add more if needed. Set aside to cool.

Use an apple corer to hollow out the courgettes, being careful not to hollow them out too much. The easiest way to do this is to push the corer 90 per cent of the way down the courgette, pull it out, then push a knife into the centre of the flesh and twist it; the core should slip out. Keep the flesh of the courgette to be used in another dish.

Stuff the courgettes with the lamb and onion mixture.

Heat the sunflower oil in another saucepan over a high heat and sear the courgettes until browned all over. Remove them from the pan and transfer the courgettes to another heavy-based saucepan. Cover with salted water and gently boil for about 20 minutes until softened and cooked through.

Use a slotted spoon to remove the courgettes from the pan. Sieve the cooking liquid to take out any meat that may have fallen out during cooking and reserve the water.

Add the yogurt to the empty pan. Add the egg and whisk together. Place over a high heat and leave it to boil and thicken for a few minutes.

Mix the cornflour with 4 tablespoons water to a paste in a bowl and add to the yogurt mix. Keep whisking until the yogurt has taken on a double cream consistency. Add about 200–240ml (7–8fl oz) of the reserved cooking liquid.

When it has all been incorporated, put the courgettes in a serving dish, pour over the yogurt sauce and serve with some Vermicelli Rice.

Warak Inab Ma' Lahme Wa Kousa
Stuffed Vine Leaves

Warak Inab is probably one of the most popular Middle Eastern dishes you will find. Making it is a labour of love. You have to get all the ingredients ready before you start and be prepared to sit in the same spot for a while. Rolling them into perfect little cigar shapes wrapped well enough not to open but not too tight to prevent the cooking process takes some skill, but after about the tenth vine leaf you will have gathered momentum and figured out how you like to do it.

Warak Inab should be made in a relaxed atmosphere, with music on in the background, recalling memories of the dish as you have eaten it before. My mother used to make this religiously when it was a birthday, Ramadan or Eid, so it holds an important place in our family's life. The tangy lemon flavour against the meaty spiced rice mix, with the fall-off-the-bone lamb cutlets is incredible. So delicious and nostalgic. The best part of all this deliciousness, is that it all gets cooked in one pot. This is the only dish my sister Maya would stop a diet for!

Serves 4–6

680ml (1lb 7oz) jar of vine
    leaves in water or brine,
    drained
500g (1lb 2oz) lamb mince
300g (10½oz) Egyptian rice
    (or pudding rice)
3 teaspoons sea salt, plus
    extra for seasoning
2 teaspoons black pepper,
    plus extra for seasoning
3 teaspoons ground
    cinnamon
2–4 tablespoons olive oil
6–8 courgettes (preferably
    Middle Eastern), cored and
    hollowed out for stuffing
    (see page 127)
2–3 beef tomatoes, cut into
    thick slices
8–10 lamb cutlets, with fat on
juice of 3 lemons
Greek yogurt and toasted
    Khubez (pita bread, see
    page 48), to serve

Begin by filling a heavy-based saucepan with boiling water. Add the vine leaves and boil for 5–8 minutes – this will help to soften the leaves and also remove any excess salt from the brine. Once softened, remove the vine leaves from the water, rinse under cold water, then leave them to drain.

Meanwhile, put the mince, rice, salt, pepper and cinnamon in a large bowl and mix together, adding the olive oil to combine fully. Taste a little to see if you need any more seasoning.

Fill each courgette two-thirds full with the rice mix, taking care not to push the mix in too forcefully, and then set aside.

Now, begin rolling. Flatten one leaf on a clean surface with the vein side up, long side nearest you. Place a thumbnail amount of rice and meat mix at the base of the leaf and spread it across the width. Begin to roll from your nearest side, then turn the edges in. Holding it securely, continue rolling upwards until it resembles a small cigar shape. Set aside and repeat with the rest of the vine leaves and stuffing.

When you have finished rolling, arrange the sliced tomato in a heavy-based saucepan to protect the dish, layering them in a ring and covering the whole base of the pan. Season the lamb cutlets with salt and pepper.

Add a layer of stuffed vine leaves and then a layer of lamb cutlets and stuffed courgettes, followed by another layer of vine leaves.

Place the saucepan on the hob and cover the vine leaves with water until it just covers the top layer of the leaves, if even that.

Place a plate over the top so that it is touching the vine leaves to prevent them from moving around and breaking. Bring to the boil and then continue to cook over a high heat for 20 minutes. Reduce to a medium-low heat for about 2½–3 hours. You must keep checking the dish throughout the cooking time to make sure the water hasn't evaporated during the first two hours and top up as needed.

About 15 minutes before the end of the cooking time, when most of the liquid should have evaporated, add the lemon juice to the pan so that it can be soaked up in the final stages.

When it is ready, take a baking tray or serving dish that is bigger than your pan and place it over the top of the pan. Carefully tip the pan upside down, holding the tray in place, to tip out the vine leaves, lamb and courgettes.

Serve with yogurt and eat quickly as they won't last long. I like to eat the vine leaves stuffed into little parcels of bread and dipped into yogurt.

Shakriyeh

Lamb Shanks Cooked in Yogurt Sauce with Burghul (Cracked Wheat) & Vermicelli

I have always loved lamb shanks, which meant that I requested them often during my childhood. My mother, being who she is, never said no. She loved cooking and loved that we adored eating her amazing food. This dish demonstrates the best of Palestinian cooking – making a little go a long way and creating delicious food out of a few ingredients. You want this dish to stay as white in colour as possible – that's the hard part of cooking this recipe. Farid, my eldest nephew, also loves lamb shanks – he likes the earthiness of the creamy yogurt sauce against the smoothness of the lamb sitting on the nutty burghul (cracked wheat) and vermicelli base. He loves to eat it with bites of fresh onion and radish – just the way I like it, too.

Serves 4

100ml (3½fl oz) sunflower oil

4–5 large onions, chopped

4 lamb shanks

2–3 teaspoons sea salt

700g (1½lb) Greek yogurt

1 egg white

3 tablespoons cornflour

sliced green pepper, radishes
   and sliced onion, to serve

For the burghul & vermicelli:

100ml (3½fl oz) vegetable oil

2 vermicelli nests, crushed

200g (7oz) coarse burghul
   (cracked wheat)

375ml (13fl oz) water

2 teaspoons sea salt

Heat the sunflower oil in a pan over a low heat and add the onions. Sauté them for 10–15 minutes until soft – it's important not to let them take on any colour.

Meanwhile, put the lamb shanks in another saucepan, cover with water and bring to the boil. Skim off any scum that may appear on the surface during this time. Continue boiling and skimming, and after about 15 minutes, remove the lamb from the water and add it to the onions. Cover with enough water to just cover the shanks and add the salt. Simmer for about 2 hours until tender.

Use a slotted spoon to remove the lamb from the cooking liquid and set it aside. Sieve the cooking liquid, reserving the stock and discarding the onions.

Put the yogurt and egg white in another saucepan. Mix the cornflour and 2–3 teaspoons water together in a small bowl to a liquidy paste. Add it to the yogurt and bring to the boil over a medium heat. Add the lamb shanks and about 175–200ml (6–7fl oz) of the reserved stock, stir together and cook for about 5–10 minutes.

To make the burghul and vermicelli, heat the vegetable oil in a saucepan and toast the crushed vermicelli. Once it has browned slightly, add the burghul (cracked wheat) and toss it around the pan, then cover with the water and season with salt. Cook over a low heat for 15 minutes.

Serve the lamb shanks with the burghul and some green pepper, radish and onions, if liked.

Artichoke Hearts with Lamb, Broad Beans & Carrots

This is a really delicious way to include vegetables in your diet. It is such a wonderful contrast of simple flavours with the minced meat and vegetables cutting through the silky smooth artichoke. I like to serve the stuffed artichoke hearts on a bed of Vermicelli Rice (see page 93) to make more of a meal out of it.

Serves 6–8

100ml (3½fl oz) sunflower oil

1 large onion, diced

500g (1lb 2oz) lamb mince

2 teaspoons ground cinnamon

2 teaspoons sea salt

1 teaspoon black pepper

5 carrots, peeled and chopped

500g (1lb 2oz) broad beans, shelled (use frozen if you cannot find fresh)

1 packet frozen artichoke hearts (at least 12 pieces)

480ml (18fl oz) water or chicken stock

Greek yogurt and lemon wedges, to serve

Preheat the oven to 180°C fan (200°C/400°F/Gas 6).

Heat the oil in a pan over a medium heat and sauté the onions until softened. Add the lamb, cinnamon, salt and pepper and continue cooking for about 6–8 minutes until the meat has browned. Set aside.

Put the carrots and beans in a deep baking tray and roughly mix together.

Put the artichoke hearts in a saucepan of salted water and bring to the boil. Continue to cook for about 10 minutes. Drain the artichokes and add them to the baking tray. Spoon the lamb into the artichoke hearts.

Add enough water or stock (about 480ml/17fl oz) to reach just halfway up the artichokes. Cover the tray with foil and bake for 40 minutes until the meat has browned and the water has reduced. Check that the artichokes have cooked through by inserting a knife; if it comes out easily, they are cooked. Serve with yogurt and a squeeze of lemon, if liked.

Tips: You can use tinned artichokes instead of the frozen ones, but you will need to omit the boiling stage as they will already be cooked and won't need to be boiled before they are baked in the oven. You could also use fresh artichokes if you prefer.

You can change this into a vegetarian dish by omitting the lamb mince and adding more chopped carrots, peas, broad beans and potatoes, to be baked with vegetable stock in a baking dish covered with foil for 35–45 minutes. You can really use any vegetable that you favour here to make it in to a delicious vegetarian dish.

Frozen artichoke hearts are found in the freezer section of most Middle Eastern shops, cleaned and ready to be cooked.

M'nasalat Betinjan
Aubergine & Mixed Lamb Bake

When my brother moved away to live in Qatar for work, we always knew he was coming home to visit when we woke up to the smell of this dish cooking. My mum would literally wake up in the middle of the night to prepare this dish so it would be ready for his arrival. I love the commitment and love she has for all of us. She always makes our favourite foods when we have been missed and I now do the same when I am missing her. So this dish is dedicated to Mo and Mama.

Serves 6

650ml (22fl oz) sunflower oil

5 large aubergines, peeled in stripes, leaving some skin intact, then sliced into 1.5cm (¾ inch) rings (see Tip)

5 onions, chopped

1 teaspoon ground cinnamon

2 teaspoons sea salt, plus extra for seasoning

1 teaspoon black pepper

500g (1lb 2oz) lamb mince

1½ tomatoes, cut in half

250–300ml (8½–10fl oz) water

radishes, sliced green peppers, green chillies, spring onions, lemon wedges and Vermicelli Rice (see page 93), to serve

Preheat the oven to 200°C fan (220°C/425°F/Gas 7).

Put 500ml (18fl oz) of the sunflower oil in a large saucepan over a high heat and fry the aubergines for 5–10 minutes until golden brown. Set aside on kitchen paper to drain any excess oil and season with salt.

Put half the remaining oil in another saucepan over a high heat and fry the onions until softened. Add the cinnamon, salt and black pepper and sauté for 10–15 minutes until they have taken on a little colour.

In a separate saucepan, brown the lamb mince in the remaining oil, stirring continuously. You want it to be broken into little pieces, so keep moving to break up the meat. Mix the lamb and onions together and set aside.

Arrange a layer of aubergine in a deep baking tray or dish – you will need more aubergines to cover the top than the bottom, so if you feel you don't have enough, spread sparingly on the base, leaving more for the top. Top with a layer of minced lamb and onions, then another layer of aubergines. Lastly, top with the tomatoes and spoon a little of the lamb mixture on top of each one.

Pour the water into the tray – you want it to reach just below the top aubergine layer. Cover the dish with foil and bake for about 45 minutes. Serve with raw vegetables, lemon wedges and Vermicelli Rice.

Tip: Half peel the aubergine by peeling off alternating strips, leaving some skin behind so that the aubergine keeps its shape during cooking.

Lahmeh Mishwiyeh
Grilled Lamb Skewers with Pomegranate Salad

My family are famous for their barbecues – we have them all through the year, come rain or shine. We make a selection of meats and salads and never forget to include my mother's *Mutabbal* (see page 102), which accompanies everything. We are meat lovers through and through and this dish really celebrates how we, as a family, eat. I love the tangy lemon and garlic flavour that permeates through the lamb and the tenderness of the meat as it falls off the skewers. It never fails to impress and there is never enough – we always fight over the last one.

Serves 4

500g (1lb 2oz) lamb
   eye-round fillet, cut into
   bite-sized pieces
juice of 2 lemons, plus
   a little extra for the salad
3 tablespoons Greek yogurt
2 garlic cloves, crushed
3 tablespoons olive oil, plus
   extra for drizzling
1 fennel bulb, shaved
1 pomelo (or orange)
1 pomegranate, seeded
a small bunch of fresh
   flat-leaf parsley
sea salt and black pepper

You will also need:

small metal skewers or
   wooden skewers that have
   been soaked in water for
   30 minutes

Put the lamb in a bowl and add the lemon juice, yogurt, crushed garlic, olive oil and some salt and pepper to taste. Leave this to marinate for at least 1 hour in the fridge – the flavours will penetrate through the meat to tenderize and create a delicious flavour.

Meanwhile, make the salad. Put the fennel in a bowl. Peel the pomelo (or orange), take out 6 segments and add them to the fennel (use the remaining segments for another dish). Add the pomegranate seeds, some parsley leaves and drizzle with some olive oil, a squeeze of lemon and season with salt.

Remove the marinated meat from the fridge and thread the lamb pieces onto the metal or soaked wooden skewers. Cook the lamb skewers under a hot grill or in a hot dry frying pan for about 3 minutes on each side (depending on how you like the meat cooked). Don't forget that marinating the meat has already started the cooking process. Once the skewers are cooked, serve and eat straightaway with a side of the fresh and tangy salad.

Tips: You can also add onions, peppers and courgettes to the skewers and grill them on a hot grill or barbecue. It's a great way to include vegetables and lots of colour! My mum used to do that when we were younger but now prefers to keep them simple as they are always accompanied by other vegetable dishes such as *Mama's Mutabbal* (see page 102) and *M'sabaha* (see page 75).

It is also a good idea to make more than you think you'll need as they are so good and you will want to eat all of them!

Shorabet Lahmeh Wa Shariyeh
Pomegranate Meatballs with a Vermicelli Tomato Soup

Another great Palestinian soup is a meatball soup seasoned with pomegranate molasses and served in a lovely thick tomato broth. My mother made this for us when we were ill and also many times during Ramadan to break our fast. It is a hearty, homely soup with so much depth of flavour that it often features on my dinner table. I always make this for friends when they are not well and suddenly they perk up from all the wonderful flavours in their mouth. Meat goes particularly well with pomegranate molasses as it breaks through the fattiness of the lamb.

Serves 4–6

1 large onion, chopped
a small bunch of fresh
    flat-leaf parsley, chopped
    (reserving some to garnish)
500g (1lb 2oz) lamb mince
2 teaspoons sea salt
1 teaspoon black pepper
2 tablespoons sunflower oil
4 tablespoons pomegranate
    molasses

For the soup:
600ml (1 pint) water
    (or chicken stock)
5 vermicelli nests, crushed
300ml (½ pint) tomato
    passata
1 teaspoon sea salt
1 teaspoon caster sugar

Mix the onions and parsley in a large bowl. Add the lamb, salt and pepper and mix together. Shape into small meatballs, varying in size, and set aside.

Heat the sunflower oil in a pan over a high heat. Add the meatballs to the pan and fry for about 10 minutes or until browned all over. Add the pomegranate molasses and stir so that the meatballs are covered in molasses and soak up the flavour. Cook for about 2 minutes.

To make the soup, put the water or chicken stock in a large saucepan and add the crushed vermicelli nests and tomato passata. Cook for about 5 minutes, then add the meatballs and the juices from the pan and let them cook in the stock for about 5–10 minutes.

Taste for seasoning – I usually add 1 teaspoon salt and 1 teaspoon sugar to balance out the acid in the tomatoes. Serve in a bowl with a small amount of chopped parsley mixed into the soup.

Malfouf

Garlic & Caraway Stuffed Cabbage Leaves

Stuffed cabbage leaves are just heavenly with the mix of caraway, lemon, oil and garlic. They can be slightly time consuming to make but it is definitely worth the effort. I like to make more than I need and put the rest in the freezer for the next time I feel like eating these juicy, tangy wraps. *Malfouf* literally means 'wrapped or rolled', which is exactly what we are going to do to these cabbage leaves. Get comfortable and relax while you are making these – they take time and attention to get right. My niece Tamara loves this dish for the sweet garlic and tangy lemon flavour against the cabbage. She also loves eating it as it reminds her of her beautiful grandmother, which makes it even more enjoyable.

Serves 6

1 Middle Eastern cabbage (see Tip) – about 1.5kg (3lb 5oz)

400g (14oz) Egyptian rice (or pudding rice)

250g (9oz) lamb mince

1 teaspoon ground cinnamon

1 teaspoon black pepper

50ml (2fl oz) olive oil

2 teaspoons sea salt

2 whole heads of garlic, 1 with skins left on and the other peeled and smashed

1 tablespoon ground caraway

350–400ml (12–14fl oz) water

juice of 3 lemons

300ml (10fl oz) Greek yogurt, to serve

Put the whole cabbage in a large saucepan of boiling water and boil for about 10 minutes to soften. Drain and leave it to cool. Start peeling the leaves from the cabbage and remove the stalk in the centre. Each piece should be no bigger than your palm, so you may need to cut it in half.

Mix the rice, lamb, cinnamon, pepper and olive oil together with the salt in a large bowl.

Place one cabbage leaf, thinnest part towards you, on a clean surface and put 1 teaspoon of the mix on this edge. Fold upwards slightly and then bring in the edges and continue to roll upwards until it looks like a small cigar shape. Repeat with the rest of the cabbage leaves and filling. If you are struggling to roll these up, you can just fold one side in as you roll, but make sure the open ends are placed against the side of the pan to help hold everything together.

Put the garlic cloves with skins in the base of a large pan and sprinkle with the caraway. Arrange the stuffed cabbage leaves on top so that they fit snugly next to each other. Scatter with the smashed garlic cloves and cover with the water. Place an upturned plate on top of the leaves in the pan to snugly hold the leaves in place and then top with the pan lid. Bring to the boil and cook for 10 minutes. Lower the heat and cook for a further 45 minutes.

Once the liquid has almost entirely evaporated, add the lemon juice, turn the temperature up to medium and cook for a further 10 minutes. Serve the *malfouf* with some yogurt and some chilli cabbage salad (see below), if liked.

Tips: With the leftover cabbage heart that can't be used for rolling, you can make a delicious salad to accompany this dish. Slice the cabbage finely and place in a bowl. Add 1 chopped red chilli, the juice of 1 lemon, a small handful of chopped fresh flat-leaf parsley, 2 tablespoons olive oil and some salt. The sharp, tangy chilli salad against the garlicky wraps is divine.

If you can't find Middle Eastern cabbage, you can use normal white cabbage or Savoy cabbage, but the leaves will be thicker and may need a few minutes more boiling to soften enough for rolling.

Fasoulia Bil Lahme

String Beans with Lamb Cooked in a Garlicky Tomato Sauce

You can make this recipe with okra, but I prefer it with string beans – some countries, Lebanon in particular, use butter beans. You may have to use a few more pans than you would like to, but the end result is just divine. Like my mother, I try to bring different foods, tastes and styles into my home, to feed my family and friends. Even if they are not used to eating it, or have never tried it, they always love the flavours. Rice is the usual accompaniment for this dish with some green chilli and green pepper. Some family traditions should never be lost and this one, I hope, will be one of those dishes that is made and remembered for its simplicity of ingredients and its greatness of flavour.

Serves 2–4

3 onions, 1 quartered and
  2 chopped

500g (1lb 2oz) lamb neck or
  lamb fillet, cubed

150ml (5fl oz) vegetable oil

1 whole head of garlic,
  cloves crushed

500g (1lb 2oz) fine string
  beans

1kg (2¼lb) tomato passata

2 tablespoons tomato purée

1 quantity of Vermicelli Rice
  (see page 93)

1 green pepper, deseeded
  and chopped

green chilli, chopped

sea salt

Fill a saucepan with boiling water, add 2 teaspoons salt and set over a high heat. Add the quartered onion and the lamb and bring to the boil. Remove any scum that appears on the surface. Keep doing this until no more scum appears. Leave it to simmer for 40 minutes.

Heat the vegetable oil in another saucepan and gently sauté the chopped onions and garlic for about 10 minutes until soft but not browned. Add the string beans, turn the heat down and let them cook gently for 15 minutes.

After about 40 minutes, remove the meat from the pan and reserve the liquid – this will make the sauce full of flavour.

Once the beans have cooked, add the passata with half the cooking liquor from the lamb. It's important that the beans are cooked before you add the tomato sauce as the acidity in the tomato will stop the beans from cooking.

Add the tomato purée and stir through. Add the meat and leave to simmer for 30 minutes over a medium heat. Check for flavour and add a little salt if needed as the tomato purée is a little sour. Continue cooking over a medium heat while you begin to cook the rice.

Cook the Vermicelli Rice as per the instructions on page 93. When it is cooked, you are ready to serve.

Place a good amount of Vermicelli Rice in a serving bowl and ladle over the terracotta-coloured lamb stew, then let it cool slightly before serving. Serve with the green pepper and chilli and eat to your heart's content.

Fatayer

Spiced Meat Parcels with Pomegranates

I know these delicious meat parcels as *fatayer*, but the flat version with the same ingredients is called *Lahm bil Ajeen*, which translated means 'meat with pastry'. These pastries are lamb-based with an infusion of spices that will bounce around your mouth. I know the ingredients list might seem long, but trust me, it only takes about 6 minutes to get both the pastry and the meat mix ready.

Makes about 24 parcels

For the pastry:

500g (1lb 2oz) plain flour, plus extra for dusting

1 teaspoon sea salt

100g (3½oz) butter, softened

1 egg yolk, plus an extra yolk for brushing

150ml (5fl oz) buttermilk

200ml (7fl oz) water

1 tablespoon dried chilli flakes

1 tablespoon cumin seeds

For the meat filling:

1 teaspoon paprika

½ teaspoon ground coriander

½ teaspoon ground cumin

1 teaspoon dried chilli flakes

1 teaspoon ground cinnamon

½ teaspoon ground nutmeg

1½ teaspoons sea salt

1 garlic clove, finely chopped

1 onion, finely chopped.

1 tablespoon pomegranate molasses

400g (14oz) lamb mince

1 pomegranate, seeded

a handful of fresh flat-leaf parsley, chopped

To make the pastry, rub the flour, salt and butter together until it resembles breadcrumbs. Add the egg yolk, buttermilk and water and combine. Before it has all come together, add the chilli flakes and cumin seeds and knead until you have a slightly smooth dough. Wrap in cling film and place in the fridge until you need it.

Preheat the oven to 200°C fan (220°C/425°F/Gas 7).

To make the meat filling, mix all the ingredients, except the pomegranate seeds and parsley, and set aside.

Remove the pastry from the fridge and turn out onto a floured surface. Cut the dough into three pieces. Roll one piece out to 5mm (⅛ inch) thick. Cut out 8cm (3¼ inch) circles and set them on a baking tray. Repeat with the other two pieces of dough. This recipe should make about 24 in total if you re-use the cuttings as you work.

Place a small teaspoon of the meat mixture and in the centre of a dough circle. Fold the edges into the centre and pinch them together to create a diamond shape, leaving some of the stuffing exposed. Repeat with the rest of the dough and meat mixture and place on baking trays. Brush the pastry edges with beaten egg.

Bake for about 12–15 minutes until golden and crisp. Scatter pomegranate seeds and some parsley on top to add some crunch and punch!

Tips: If you find the filling and shaping of the dough circles too difficult, you can just roll out 6–8 small circles and top with the lamb mixture like you would pizza. These are called *Lahm bil Ajeen* (as mentioned above), and are just as authentic and delicious.

This spiced meat can also be used to replace *sujuk* (spicy sausage) in recipes if you can't find it, such as the Spicy Lamb Sausage with Scrambled Eggs on page 26.

Betinjan Wa Kousa Mehshi
Stuffed Aubergine & Courgette with Lamb in a Tomato Broth

Betinjan Mehshi means 'stuffed aubergine' but this dish can be made with either Middle Eastern courgettes or aubergines, or both if you fancy it. Aubergines have a smoky flavour to them that turns any dish into something special. As you might have gathered, I think my mother's recipes are wonderful. She gets so passionate about telling me the recipe and often gets her sisters involved, so when I ask her about measurements for salt or a spice, it turns into a huge discussion with her sisters about who uses more of this and that and in the end it all boils down to what she says . . . well for me anyway. I sometimes make this fantastic dish in advance as it always tastes better after a few hours, so make sure you do that whenever you are short on time.

Serves 4–6

4 aubergines

4 courgettes (preferably
    Middle Eastern) (optional)

300g (10½oz) lamb mince

175g (6oz) Egyptian rice
    (or pudding rice)

3 teaspoons sea salt

1 teaspoon black pepper

3 teaspoons ground
    cinnamon

10 tomatoes (or 1 litre/1¾
    pints tomato passata)

3 tablespoons tomato purée

green peppers and green
    chillies, chopped, to serve

Cut the tops off the aubergines and courgettes, if using, and hollow out the insides, being sure not to puncture the skin.

Mix the mince with the rice in a large bowl and season with salt, pepper and cinnamon. Be quite robust with the seasoning, otherwise you may end up with a very bland dish.

Fill the aubergines and courgettes, if using, with meat and rice, but do not force the mixture in. Tap it gently on the base to let it settle and leave a gap at the top for the rice to swell as it cooks.

Chop and whiz the tomatoes in a food processor or blender, then pour them into a deep saucepan over a medium heat and bring to a simmer. Add the tomato purée, then add the stuffed vegetables. Make sure they are at least three-quarters covered with the tomato sauce and add water if needed. I love the way they resemble whales swimming in a bubbling lava-coloured ocean!

Bring to the boil and keep cooking over a high heat for about 15 minutes. Turn the heat down to a medium-low and continue cooking for about 1 hour. Remove the stuffed vegetables from the pan and serve, drizzling the tomato sauce all over, with green peppers and chilli, if liked. You will definitely feel stuffed after this, but in a good way!

Tip: You can substitute the lamb for beef mince, if preferred.

Spiced Lamb Ribs

I made this dish by accident while trying to recreate something my mother had made. Sometimes memories can be so strong that they create wonderful recipes.

Serves 4

2 aubergines, cubed

1 teaspoon ground cinnamon

1 teaspoon dried chilli flakes

1 teaspoon ground nutmeg

1 teaspoon smoked paprika

1 teaspoon ground ginger

1 teaspoon ground cumin

2 teaspoons dried mint

16 lamb ribs

1 tablespoon olive oil

juice of ½ lemon

sea salt

2 tablespoons Greek yogurt

Preheat the oven to 220°C fan (240°C/465°F/Gas 9).

Put the aubergines on a baking tray and drizzle with a little oil and salt.

Mix all the spices together (reserving half the mint), then rub them onto the lamb ribs, adding the oil, lemon juice and salt.

Place the ribs on top of the aubergines and bake for about 20 minutes, or more if you like the lamb well cooked.

Mix the yogurt and the reserved mint together in a bowl. Eat the ribs with your hands and some flat *khubez* (pita bread, see page 48) to help soak up all the flavours and the mint yogurt on the side for dipping.

Tip: I often sprinkle a pinch of cayenne pepper over the ribs before eating for an extra kick.

Jawaneh
Chilli Chicken Wings

When we were younger we used to go to a Middle Eastern restaurant every Sunday. This was the dish we ordered the most – we would eat dozens of them, tray after tray after tray.

Serves 4

5 garlic cloves, crushed

1 red chilli, chopped

1 tablespoon Greek yogurt

100ml (3½fl oz) olive oil

1 tablespoon sea salt

1 teaspoon za'atar

1 teaspoon cayenne pepper

1 teaspoon sumac

2 lemons

2 fresh thyme sprigs

20 chicken wings

Mix the garlic, chilli, yogurt, oil, salt, za'atar, cayenne and sumac together in a bowl. Squeeze in the juice from the lemons (and add in the squeezed skins too). Add the leaves from the thyme sprigs. Add the chicken wings and mix everything together so that the chicken is well coated. Leave to marinate for about 2 hours if you have time. If not, you can cook them straightaway, but they will not have the same intensity of flavour.

Preheat the oven to 200°C fan (220°C/425°F/Gas 7).

Once marinated, place the chicken wings on a baking tray and bake for about 25–35 minutes until they have charred slightly. Enjoy straightaway.

Tip: The wings can also be cooked on a hot barbecue for 15 minutes.

Djaj Mehshi
Poussin Stuffed with Spiced Mince & Egyptian Rice

I love autumn, purely for the comfort food that we are now 'allowed' to eat. Of course we can eat these things any time but it just feels right to eat these dishes when the weather has turned and the nights are starting to draw in. During Ramadan and family get togethers we always cook *Djaj Mehshi* (meaning 'stuffed chicken'). It is so simple – which is the best part about it – just two stages and you're done. The only thing I would suggest is to make sure you season everything really well to retain plenty of flavour in the final cooking stages.

Serves 4–8

100ml (3½fl oz) olive oil

250g (9oz) lamb mince

3 teaspoons ground nutmeg

4 teaspoons ground cinnamon

200g (7oz) Egyptian rice (or pudding or basmati rice)

4 poussins

2 onions, roughly chopped

sea salt and black pepper

Greek yogurt, to serve

Preheat the oven to 190°C fan (210°C/415°F/Gas 6–7).

Heat the oil in a pan over a high heat, add the lamb mince and season with half the nutmeg and half the cinnamon and some salt and pepper. You will want the meat to colour well and cook most of the way through.

Add the rice to the lamb and mix together until it is all combined and the rice has been slightly toasted. Add enough water to cover the rice by just a knuckle's depth and stir through. Taste the water to check for seasoning as you may have to add more – if it tastes simply of water, add more cinnamon, nutmeg, salt and pepper.

Let the mixture cook for about 10–12 minutes until three-quarters done (it will continue to cook in the oven), then take the pan off the heat and leave it to cool slightly.

Once it has cooled, stuff the poussin with the filling, then close the legs and tie with string to stop the filling from spilling out. Season the poussin all over with the remaining nutmeg and cinnamon and some salt and pepper and place them in a shallow baking dish. Add enough water to come halfway up the sides of the dish, then add the onions.

Cover the dish with foil and bake in the oven for 60–70 minutes, removing the foil halfway through the cooking time to get a lovely crisp finish.

Use the cooking liquid in the dish to drizzle over the chicken and serve with Greek yogurt.

Fatet' Djaj
Chicken Pita Yogurt Bake

During the holiday season my family usually cooks all the normal festive dishes, but we also go all out with Arabic dishes that are, to me, just sublime. You can make this dish with aubergines, chickpeas, chicken, lamb – it really is very versatile. This dish is made up of layers and must be eaten straightaway due to the hot liquid and yogurt that is poured over the crisp pita bread. The flavour of the chicken and lamb mince (which is quite rich) and the rice (which is smooth) hitting the tangy yogurt and crunchy pita makes all the senses explode in your mouth.

Serves 6–8

1 medium whole chicken

10 cardamom pods

1 onion, cut into quarters

1 tablespoon sea salt, plus
  extra for seasoning

100ml (3½fl oz) vegetable oil

250g (9oz) lamb mince

2 teaspoons ground nutmeg

2 teaspoons ground
  cinnamon

400g (14oz) Egyptian rice (or
  pudding or basmati rice)

650ml (22fl oz) water

2 x 500g (1lb 2oz) tubs Greek
  yogurt

3 garlic cloves, crushed

2 green chillies, chopped

juice of 1 lemon

5–6 thick pita bread

a small bunch of fresh
  flat-leaf parsley, chopped

50g (1¾oz) toasted pine nuts

50g (1¾oz) toasted almonds

black pepper

Put the chicken in a saucepan of water with the cardamom pods, onion and salt, and bring to the boil. Leave to cook at a rolling, rumbling boil for about 75 minutes.

Heat the oil in a separate saucepan over a medium heat and fry the lamb mince. Season well with salt, pepper, nutmeg and cinnamon. Cook until the mince is very well browned. Add the rice to the pan and toast for a minute or so. Add the water and bring to the boil. Taste the water to check that you've added enough seasoning – you should be able to taste all the flavours. Continue cooking for 15–18 minutes over a medium-low heat until the liquid has evaporated and you are left with slightly sticky, puffy rice.

Meanwhile, make the yogurt sauce. Empty the yogurt into a bowl, add the garlic and chilli and mix well. Add a squeeze of lemon juice and some salt to taste. It should be tart, garlicky, lemony and salted. Transfer to the fridge to marinate for up to 1 hour.

Preheat the oven to 180°C fan (200°C/400°F/Gas 6).

Cut the pita into triangles and place them on a baking tray. Bake them in the oven for about 7–8 minutes to toast – or you can fry them like my mother does. Once toasted, remove from the oven and leave to cool.

When the chicken has cooked, drain, reserving the water, and shred the meat.

Once all the food has cooked, you can begin layering. Toasted pita is first into the dish. Add about 300ml (½ pint) of the reserved stock to the yogurt – not too much as you want the flavour of both the yogurt and stock to come through. Pour this over the pita, and quickly add the shredded chicken, then spoon over the lamb rice. Top with the chopped parsley and toasted nuts and eat straightaway.

Tip: You can substitute the chicken with 800g (1lb 12oz) lamb neck and cook in the same way, shredding the meat once it has cooked.

Mussakhan – Auntie Lamia's Way
Chicken Cooked with Sumac, Olive Oil & Onions

Mussakhan, one of the national dishes of Palestine, is just one of those dishes that you can't stop eating once you have started. You absolutely have to eat it with your hands – none of this silly fork and knife business please! – the flavour is just more exaggerated when eaten by hand. In Ramallah, in Palestine, they have just submitted the largest *mussakhan*, which has been accepted in to the Guinness Book of Records. It is more than 4 metres (13 feet) long and weighs more than 1,350kg (2,976lb) – I would love to have a bite of that! This is a very simple, hearty, full-of-flavour dish that you must try. It should be very oniony and dripping with olive oil. The sumac really is the star of the show and turns the bread a beautiful magenta colour. Auntie Lamia always used to make this when she was coming to the end of her visit to London, before going back home to Palestine – it was always her farewell dish.

Serves 6-8

1 whole large chicken, skin on and cut into 4–6 pieces

5 cardamom pods

2 tablespoons sea salt

550–650ml (19–22fl oz) olive oil

12–14 onions, chopped

1 teaspoon ground cumin

½ teaspoon black pepper

½ teaspoon ground cinnamon

150g (5½oz) sumac

4–6 flat breads

75g (2¾oz) toasted pine nuts

75g (2¾oz) toasted almonds

fresh flat-leaf parsley, chopped, to serve

Put the chicken in a saucepan of water with the cardamom and 1 tablespoon of the salt and boil for 1 hour.

Heat the oil in a frying pan and sauté the onions, remaining salt, cumin, black pepper and cinnamon for about 45 minutes over a low heat until completely soft but not browned.

Preheat the oven to 220°C fan (240°C/465°F/Gas 9).

Once the chicken has boiled, remove it from the water (you can keep the stock and use it for another recipe, if liked).

Place about 1 tablespoon of the cooked onions onto each piece of chicken and sprinkle some sumac over the top of each one. Place the chicken pieces on a baking tray and bake for 5 minutes until slightly browned on top.

Slather each flat bread with onions, scatter generously with sumac, adding bits of chicken and some toasted nuts and parsley to each one. Repeat for all the remaining breads and pieces of chicken and serve. Rip pieces of bread with the chicken, get messy and eat with your hands.

Molokhia
Jute Mallow Cooked Two Ways

Molokhia (jute mallow) is one of dozens of names for the leafy plant of the Corchorus species, which is commonly used in Palestinian, Egyptian and other Middle Eastern cooking. It is known to be the food of Kings and Pharoahs in Egypt (the word *molouk* means 'king or royalty'). It has a wonderfully relaxing and comforting effect when you eat it. My sister Tania often makes this to remind her of her childhood. I often cook these two *molokhia* dishes at the same time as they are so easy to make and it is nice to enjoy the two different dishes served together.

Serves 4

1 whole chicken

1–1.5 litres (1¾–2⅔ pints)
    water

1 large onion, quartered

4 cardamom pods

1 x 400g (14oz) packet frozen
    molokhia (jute mallow),
    smooth

50ml (2fl oz) olive oil

4 garlic cloves, crushed

1 quantity of Vermicelli Rice
    (see page 93)

sea salt and black pepper

toasted *Khubez* (pita bread,
    see page 48) and lemon
    wedges, to serve

For the dressing:

2 shallots, finely diced

1 green chilli, chopped

3 tablespoons red wine
    vinegar

Put the chicken in a large saucepan with 500ml (18fl oz) of the water, the onion and cardamom pods. Season with salt and pepper, bring to the boil, lower the heat to a simmer and cook for about 1 hour. Strain and reserve the stock, pouring 500ml (18fl oz) into a clean saucepan. Shred the chicken meat and set aside.

Add the *molokhia* (jute mallow) to the chicken stock, bring to the boil and then reduce the heat to a simmer for about 15 minutes.

While the *molokhia* is cooking, heat the olive oil in a pan over a medium heat and cook the garlic until slightly browned. Add this to the *molokhia* and mix.

Mix all the dressing ingredients together in a small bowl and season with salt. Divide the Vermicelli Rice between four serving bowls and top each bowl with *molokhia* soup and some shredded chicken. Drizzle over some dressing and serve with *khubez* (pita bread).

Tips: Use 4 chicken breasts instead of a whole chicken if you are short on time, and only cook for 20 minutes to make the chicken stock.

You can also make a dry version of this dish, also known as *Molokhia Warak*. Heat 50ml (2fl oz) olive oil in a saucepan over a medium to high heat and sauté 1 large chopped onion and 1 whole head of peeled and sliced garlic cloves for about 10 minutes, until softened but not browned. Add 1 sliced green chilli and 250g (9oz) fresh *molokhia* leaves or 400g (14oz) frozen and thawed leaves and sauté together for several minutes. Add 250ml (9fl oz) chicken stock and 1 teaspoon salt and cook for about 10–12 minutes, until the leaves have soaked up all the liquid and are completely soft. Serve with *khubez* (pita breads) and lots of lemon juice squeezed on top.

Za'atar Chicken
Chicken Marinated with Za'atar, Chilli & Pomegranate Molasses

This dish, or a similar version, is eaten all over Palestine. I love za'atar, but as much as I love it, it can be a little overwhelming. The best za'atar can be found in Middle Eastern shops or online stores. Inferior quality za'atar will make your food taste woody and bitter so always go for the best quality you can find.

This dish came about when I ran my restaurant, Baity Kitchen. I had some chicken legs in the fridge that needed using up and wanted something punchy and colourful. This dish became a staple in my restaurant for three years – never changing, and with an ever-increasing crowd who would reserve a piece every day. I still make this all the time. It triggers good memories, makes me feel good and I love how the amazing flavours just explode in my mouth.

Serves 4

4 large chicken leg and
   thigh pieces
olive oil, for drizzling
4 tablespoons dried mint
5 tablespoons pomegranate
   molasses
1 teaspoon dried red chilli
   flakes
4 teaspoons za'atar
   (see page 17)
1 teaspoon sea salt
1 pomegranate, seeded
1 red chilli, sliced
fresh mint leaves, to garnish

Preheat the oven to 180°C fan (200°C/400°F/Gas 6) and line a baking tray with baking parchment. Drizzle the chicken pieces with olive oil to lightly coat the skin and place them, skin side down, on the lined tray. Sprinkle half of all the flavourings over the top, except for the pomegranate seeds, chilli slices and mint leaves, then turn over and sprinkle over the remainder. Turn the chicken again so it is now facing skin side down.

Bake in the oven for 10 minutes. Once the chicken has browned slightly, turn the pieces over and cook skin side up for a further 10 minutes. If you feel you need to add more of any of the flavourings, please do – I usually add a little more za'atar and a bit more mint at this stage. Make sure that the chicken is evenly covered in all the flavourings – you want it to have a nice colour all over and flavour once it is cooked.

When the chicken is cooked, remove it from the oven and sprinkle with the pomegranate seeds and the sliced chilli. Generously drizzle the juices from the baking tray all over the chicken and garnish with mint leaves.

Tip: It is a good idea to get your chicken from a butcher to make sure you get the correct cut of meat (the leg and thigh in one whole piece rather than separated), and also ones of a good size. Otherwise you will feel utterly disappointed that it ended too soon.

Shorabet Djaj Wa Khudar
Chicken & Vegetable Soup

We all know how good chicken soup is for you, and this recipe is no different. My mother, and her mother before her, used to make this simple but delicious soup with a gorgeous hint of cardamom permeating through it. The cardamom is really the star of the show for me and is what makes this soup stand out from all the others. Family traditions are very important to me and I make this exactly the way my mother did. When I'm poorly or simply missing her, this is one of my go-to dishes, which immediately makes me feel better.

Serves 6–8

1 tablespoon sunflower oil

2 large onions, quartered

10 cardamom pods

1 teaspoon black
   peppercorns

1 whole chicken

2 litres (3½ pints) water

2 teaspoons sea salt

5 potatoes (I use King
   Edwards), peeled and
   quartered

5 carrots, peeled and cut
   lengthways and then in
   half again

½ Savoy cabbage, finely
   sliced

Put the oil in a saucepan and heat over a high heat. Add the onions, cardamom pods and peppercorns and let the cardamom sizzle slightly to release its flavour.

After a few minutes, add the whole chicken and cover with the water and salt. Leave to boil for about 30 minutes (or 50 minutes if you have a large chicken), then add the potatoes and carrots and cook for another 30 minutes, adding the sliced cabbage in the last 5 minutes. Check the meat to make sure it is cooked through before serving.

I normally carve the meat into 6–8 pieces to serve, but you could also shred the meat and remove all the bones if you prefer.

Tip: After we have eaten this soup, my mum usually turns any leftovers into another type of soup for the next day. She would shred the remaining chicken, add the veg, and toss it in a pot adding black peppercorns, a handful of Egyptian rice and some parsley and let it cook with some more stock until it is thick and the rice has cooked. It is utterly gorgeous, really soothing and easy to make using up the leftovers.

Mashbous – Auntie Noha's Recipe
Loomi (Dried Limes) & Spiced Chicken Rice Platter

This is not a particularly Palestinian dish, but is commonly made in Palestine and cooked by many of my relatives and my mother. It is from the Gulf region in the Middle East, mainly Kuwait, and has influences from India and Asia. It is spiced and fragrant and the addition of the *loomi* (dried limes) is incredible.

Serves 6

150ml (3½fl oz) sunflower oil

1 whole chicken, cut into
6–8 pieces, skin on

2 onions, chopped

2 tablespoons sea salt

2 tomatoes, chopped

2 tablespoons tomato purée

1 whole head of garlic,
cloves crushed

5 *loomi* (dried limes) pierced

1 thumb-sized piece of
fresh ginger, peeled and
chopped

5 cardamom pods

1 cinnamon stick

1 teaspoon ground cumin

1 teaspoon ground
coriander

1 teaspoon ground
cinnamon

1 teaspoon ground ginger

1 teaspoon black pepper

700ml (1¼ pints) water

350–400g (12–14oz) basmati
rice

a large bunch of fresh
coriander, leaves roughly
chopped

a large bunch of fresh flat-
leaf parsley, leaves roughly
chopped

50g (1¾oz) toasted pine
nuts, to garnish

Heat the oil in a saucepan over a high heat. Add the chicken, skin side down, and cook until browned. Use a slotted spoon to remove the chicken pieces and set them aside.

Add the onions to the hot pan and sauté for 5 minutes until softened. Add all the remaining ingredients, except the water, rice and herbs, and stir to release all the flavours. Cook, stirring, for about 5 minutes.

Return the chicken to the pan, cover with the water and leave to cook for about 20–30 minutes.

Once the chicken is cooked through, use a slotted spoon to remove it from the pan and set aside, keeping it warm.

Add the rice to the pan – scoop out some stock if it looks like you have too much in the pan; you will need enough to cover the rice by just a knuckle's depth. Add the chopped coriander and parsley and mix through. Set over a low-medium heat and cook for about 20 minutes.

When the rice is ready the liquid should have evaporated and been soaked up by the rice. Tip the rice out onto a serving platter, top with the chicken and the toasted pine nuts and serve immediately.

Fragrant Fish

Palestinians love to eat fish. It is most commonly eaten in Gaza and Yaffa as they are by the coast and have access to the water for fishing. They eat squid stuffed with freekeh, garlic and chilli prawns in a tomato sauce with arak, and *samakeh harrah* (a spicy fish dish cooked whole in the oven). The reason they use plenty of spice in this region is because they are on the spice route that used to run from the Far East, through Arabia to the Mediterranean and therefore have spice in abundance. The Gazan region is a very poor part of the country but you'll still find many delicious, wonderful dishes that will tantalize your tastebuds. Fish is usually eaten grilled or lightly fried and in this chapter you will discover some wonderfully fragrant and punchy dishes.

Sayyadiyeh

Cumin & Lemon Cod Served on Cumin Rice with Caramelized Onions & Tahini Tarator Sauce

Sayyadiyeh is the Middle Eastern version of British fish and chips. Okay, there are no chips in this dish but it is very traditional in our country to eat this. The fish is beautifully marinated and shallow fried to create this fragrant tangy taste and served alongside this almost smoky rice with a nutty tahini sauce. My mother makes this only when the whole family is together. I don't know why, but I presume it is because it is a bit of a showstopper dish. It reminds me of home and of my family and sitting around together, chatting and seeing who would end up with the biggest piece of fish when I was growing up. I love the tahini sauce, called Tarator – I dip bread into it and just eat it straight out of the bowl, it's so good!

Serves 4

3 teaspoons cumin seeds

3 teaspoons ground cumin

juice of 2 lemons

6 tablespoons olive oil

4 x 200–225g (7–8oz) cod
    fillets, with skin on

3 onions, sliced

300g (10½oz) basmati rice

3 tablespoons plain flour

4 tablespoons vegetable oil

sea salt and black pepper

mint leaves and lemon
    wedges, to garnish

For the Tarator sauce:

4 tablespoons tahini (see
    page 21)

2 tablespoons Greek yogurt

juice of 3 lemons

3 tomatoes, chopped

a bunch of fresh flat-leaf
    parsley, chopped

Mix half the cumin seeds and ground cumin with the lemon juice and 4 tablespoons of the olive oil in a small bowl. Put the cod in a dish, pour the cumin mixture all over and leave to marinate in the fridge for at least 2 hours.

Heat the remaining olive oil in a large saucepan and add the onions and the remaining cumin seeds and ground cumin. Mix and cook for 10 minutes until golden.

Add the rice to the pan and mix well to get everything coated. Pour enough water into the pan to come about 3cm (1¼ inches) above the rice and bring to the boil. Check for seasoning, then turn the heat down to a simmer and cook for a further 15 minutes.

To make the sauce, mix the tahini and yogurt with the lemon juice. Add a splash of water if the sauce seems a bit too thick. Season and add the tomatoes and parsley.

Preheat the oven to 180°C fan (200°C/400°F/Gas 6).

Take the fish out of the marinade, gently shaking off any excess liquid. Lightly coat the fish fillets in the flour and set aside.

Heat the vegetable oil for shallow frying in a frying pan. Dust any excess flour from the fish and place it, skin side down, in the pan. Cook for 3 minutes on each side.

Transfer to the oven to cook for 5–7 minutes – keep checking to make sure it is not over- or undercooked – you want the fish to be slightly crisped and browned. When ready, place the rice on a plate and surround with the fish, drizzle with the sauce and garnish with mint leaves and lemon wedges for squeezing.

Saffron & Lemon Cod with Jewelled Herby Rice

When I ran my restaurant I was always changing the menu, particularly the fish dishes. I liked to experiment with recipes I had grown up with and also take on board suggestions from my customers. One day, somebody put in a request for saffron lemon cod with rice. I called my mother immediately and she said that she knew a very similar dish and gave me the recipe to try. It was lovely, so it appeared many times on the menu.

Serves 4

4 x 250g (9oz) pieces of
    deboned cod fillets
a pinch of saffron
juice of 1 lemon
2 tablespoons olive oil
juice of ½ small orange
1 tablespoon melted butter
1 teaspoon sea salt

For the rice:
250g (9oz) basmati rice
500ml (18fl oz) water
2 teaspoons sea salt
grated zest of 1 lemon
a small bunch of fresh
    flat-leaf parsley
a small bunch of fresh chives
1–2 red chillies, chopped
1 pomegranate, seeded

For the dressing:
juice of 2 lemons
4 tablespoons olive oil
1 teaspoon sea salt
1 teaspoon caster sugar

Put the cod fillets on a baking tray. Mix the saffron, lemon juice, olive oil, orange juice, melted butter and salt in a bowl. Pour this over the cod and then transfer the fish to the fridge to marinate for 30 minutes.

Preheat the oven to 200°C fan (220°C/425°F/Gas 7).

Put the rice, water and salt in a saucepan and cook over a high heat for about 5 minutes. Add half the lemon zest, reduce the heat to low and cook for another 10–12 minutes until the rice is cooked.

Chop all the herbs and mix them together with the chillies and pomegranate seeds in a large bowl.

Once the rice is cooked, transfer it to a bowl and mix through the herbs and pomegranate seeds and the remaining lemon zest. Check for seasoning and add a little more salt or some olive oil if needed.

Bake the cod for about 10–12 minutes, checking that it doesn't overcook.

Mix the dressing ingredients together in a small bowl and stir this through the rice salad. Spoon the rice onto a serving plate and top with a cod slice, drizzling the cooking juices from the pan over the top.

Samak Meshwi Wa Batata Harra
Halibut Baked Over Spicy Potatoes

This combination of fish and spicy potatoes is amazing and it is very Mediterranean in flavour. This version of *batata harra* is slightly different to the recipe on page 97 and is a better accompaniment to fish. The potato here is sliced instead of cubed to make a base for the fish and I have used parsley instead of coriander. Halibut is one of my favourite fish to eat – it has a lovely meaty texture to complement the chilli, lemon and garlic potatoes.

Serves 4

2 large potatoes, skin on
    and finely sliced
3 garlic cloves, crushed
1 red chilli, chopped
175ml (6fl oz) olive oil
2 plum tomatoes, deseeded
    and diced
a small bunch of fresh
    flat-leaf parsley, chopped
juice of 1 lemon
1–2 teaspoons sea salt
4 x 225g (8oz) halibut fillets

Preheat the oven to 200°C fan (220°C/425°F/Gas 7).

Layer the potatoes, overlapping each other, all over the base of an ovenproof frying pan or roasting dish.

Mix the garlic, chilli, olive oil, tomatoes, parsley and lemon juice together, then pour about three-quarters of it onto the potatoes and sprinkle with a little salt. Bake for about 20 minutes, then remove from the oven.

Add the halibut to the pan on top of the potatoes and drizzle with the rest of the garlic mixture. If you don't have enough, then just make a little more – you need enough to coat the fish fillets lightly. Bake again for another 10–12 minutes. Remove from the oven, sprinkle with some salt and serve.

Sultan Ibrahim Wa Ful
Fried Red Mullet with Broad Beans & Garlic

Sultan Ibrahim (red mullet) is one of the most important fish used in Palestinian cooking. I serve this red mullet simply shallow-fried whole with a smashed bean and garlic base. Always go for smaller fish wherever possible, as they have a much better flavour.

Serves 4

4 x small red mullet, each
    weighing about 375g
    (13oz), gutted and scaled
juice of ½ lemon, plus extra
    to serve
2 teaspoons olive oil, plus
    extra to serve
1 teaspoon sea salt, plus
    extra to serve
plain flour, seasoned with
    sea salt, for dusting
250ml (9fl oz) sunflower oil

For the beans:

4 tablespoons olive oil, plus a
    little extra if needed
1 banana shallot, finely
    diced
1 garlic clove, crushed
500g (1lb 2oz) shelled broad
    beans (frozen if you can't
    find fresh)
75ml (2¾fl oz) water
1 tomato, deseeded and
    diced
a small bunch of fresh
    flat-leaf parsley
1 teaspoon sea salt (or more
    to taste)
juice of ½ lemon

Place the fish in a shallow dish and make 3–4 incisions in the skin on one side. Squeeze the lemon juice all over, drizzle with the olive oil and sprinkle with salt. Leave to marinate in the fridge for 20 minutes.

Meanwhile, begin preparing the beans. Heat the oil in a pan set over a medium heat, add the shallot and sauté for about 3 minutes. Add the garlic, then stir for a minute or so.

Add the beans and cook for about 1 minute to take on the flavour of the shallots and garlic, then add the water and continue cooking for 5 minutes. Smash the beans with a potato masher – don't mash to a purée though, you want to keep the texture chunky.

Take the pan off the heat, add the tomatoes, parsley and season with salt and lemon juice. Add some olive oil to balance out the citrus flavour if needed.

Put the seasoned flour for the fish in a shallow dish. Dust the red mullet lightly with flour all over, tapping off any excess flour as you dust.

Heat the oil in a frying pan over a high heat and shallow fry the fish for about 3–4 minutes on each side. Use a slotted spoon to remove the fish once cooked, and leave to drain on kitchen paper. Squeeze over some more lemon juice, drizzle with the extra olive oil and season with salt.

Place the smashed beans on a plate and top with the fish, finishing with a squeeze of lemon before serving.

Sultan Ibrahim Makli Wa Salatet Adas
Fried Red Mullet with Preserved Lemon & Lentil Salad

Red mullet is a popular fish for shallow frying in Arab cuisine, as it exudes such a glorious flavour. The beauty of it is that you don't need to cook it for very long either as the fillets are very thin and their red skins crisp up beautifully. The creamy lentils against the preserved sharp, tangy lemon with the crisp red mullet are a great combination here.

Serves 4

8 x red mullet fillets or
    4 x small whole fish,
    gutted and scaled
juice of 2 lemons
1 teaspoon ground cumin
400ml (14fl oz) vegetable oil
150g (5½oz) seasoned plain
    flour
sea salt and black pepper

For the lentils:
350g (12oz) puy lentils
1 shallot
1 bay leaf
1 tablespoon ground cumin
600ml (1 pint) water, and
    more if needed
4 spring onions, sliced into
    thin rings
2 tomatoes, deseeded and
    diced
1 preserved lemon, sliced
    and then into quarters,
    removing any seeds you
    may find
a bunch of fresh flat-leaf
    parsley, roughly chopped
50ml (2fl oz) white wine
    vinegar
juice of 2 lemons
200ml (7fl oz) olive oil
1–2 teaspoons sea salt

Begin by seasoning the fish with salt and pepper, squeezing over the lemon juice and sprinkling over the cumin. Place the fish in the fridge while you prepare the lentils.

Put the lentils, shallot, bay leaf and cumin in a saucepan with the water so that it covers the lentils by at least 5cm (2 inches) as the lentils will swell and soak up the water. Don't season with salt yet as this will slow the cooking process. Cook over a medium heat for about 20–25 minutes.

Meanwhile, mix the spring onion, tomato, preserved lemon and parsley in a bowl and set aside.

Once the lentils have cooked, drain and rinse them in warm water. It is best if they are still warm when you add the dressing so that they will soak up the flavours. Mix in the onion and tomato mix and then add the vinegar, lemon juice, olive oil and salt.

Pour the vegetable oil for frying the fish into a non-stick saucepan over a medium-high heat. Take the fish out of the fridge and lightly dust each one in the seasoned flour. Fry the fillets in the oil, one or two at a time, for about 1 minute on each side until cooked through – if using the whole fish the cooking time will depend on their size, but if they are small, about 2½ minutes on each side. It's really up to you to judge what looks right – they should crisp up and turn golden brown.

Serve the crispy fish on a bed of the lentils.

Tip: I sometimes finely chop the preserved lemons for the dressing instead of adding them in bigger chunks.

Samakeh Harrah
Sea Bream Served with a Spicy Red Sauce

Samakeh Harrah is one of those iconic dishes that is eaten all over the Middle East, but everyone has a different way of making it. I have spoken to my aunties, my mother and cousins and not one had the same version of this dish. One version was with tahini, one with chilli and nuts, the other with plenty of herbs and chilli. So I went with the very delicious spicy, herby, garlicky version that my mother and I make.

Serves 4

50ml (2fl oz) sunflower oil

1 small onion, chopped

1 green chilli, sliced

5 garlic cloves, sliced

a bunch of fresh coriander, chopped

1 teaspoon paprika

1 teaspoon ground cumin

juice of 2 lemons

50ml (2fl oz) olive oil

1 tomato, chopped

a pinch of black pepper

2 teaspoons sea salt

2 x sea bream, gutted and scaled

Preheat the oven to 190°C fan (210°C/415°F/Gas 6–7).

Heat the sunflower oil in a frying pan over a high heat and fry the onions, chilli and garlic for about 8 minutes until softened and slightly browned. Use a slotted spoon to transfer the contents to another bowl and set them aside.

Add the coriander, paprika, cumin, lemon juice, olive oil and chopped tomato to the same pan, season with the salt and pepper and mix together. Cook over a low heat for about 2 minutes, then add the fried onions back to the pan and stir through.

Use a sharp knife to make some small incisions along the top of the fish. Stuff the cavities of both fish with about two-thirds of the filling. Place them on a baking tray and massage the fish all over with the rest of the mixture, making sure to rub into the incisions you have made.

Bake the fish for about 15–20 minutes, depending on the size of your fish. Serve with rice, if liked, or just enjoy on its own. You can also top the fish with toasted pine nuts for an added extra touch.

Sumac & Za'atar Roasted Monkfish

Sumac and za'atar is such a wonderfully tangy and earthy combination. I make this all the time, especially with monkfish as it has such a meaty texture. This dish needs something with a little kick to break up the thickness of flavour, so I always serve it with my delicious *Salatet Fattoush* (see page 112) on the side. The reason this works so well is that you have the sharpness of sumac and lemon against the smokiness and spice of paprika and chilli. These flavours work really well in a number of dishes, but especially with fish.

Serves 4

4 x 350g (12oz) monkfish tails

4 tablespoons olive oil

4 teaspoons sumac

4 teaspoons za'atar
  (see page 17)

2 teaspoons sea salt

4 teaspoons lemon zest

juice of 1 lemon

2 teaspoons cayenne
  pepper

2 teaspoons sweet paprika

2 teaspoons dried chilli flakes

2 bunches of fresh coriander,
  chopped

Salatet Fattoush (see page
  112), to serve

Preheat the oven to 180°C fan (200°C/400°F/Gas 6). Place the monkfish on a baking tray.

Mix all the other ingredients together and season to taste – you may want to add more salt or lemon. Rub the mixture all over the monkfish so that it is evenly coated and place the squeezed lemon halves on the tray.

Bake for 12–15 minutes, or longer depending on the size of the fish, checking to make sure it doesn't overcook. When it's ready, remove and serve with *Salatet Fattoush*.

Whole Sea Bass with a Chilli Coriander Dressing

We love fish in my family and used to eat it often as I was growing up, cooked in many different ways. My mother and I loved to make whole roasted sea bass with a spicy coriander lemon sauce to drizzle on top. The mixture of spices is incredible. This combination is almost the umami of flavours in Palestinian food as it works so well with everything – I use it on meat dishes, chicken, fish, and salads. You can really feel the Middle East in your mouth and it evokes memories of days spent lying in the sun by the beach for me.

Serves 2–4

2 whole medium sea bass, gutted and scaled

150ml (5fl oz) olive oil, plus extra for drizzling

6 lemons

1 large green chilli

2 garlic cloves

a small bunch of fresh coriander

sea salt and black pepper

Preheat the oven to 180°C fan (200°C/400°F/Gas 6) and line a baking tray with baking parchment or foil.

Place the sea bass in the tray and season with salt and pepper. Drizzle with olive oil and squeeze the juice of 2 of the lemons over and inside the fish.

Make a dressing by blitzing the remaining lemon juice with the chilli, garlic, coriander and olive oil in a blender and season to taste. Add more oil and salt to taste if needed. The dressing should be a paste consistency that is a little runny. You can mix it in a pestle and mortar if you don't have a blender.

Rub one-third of the paste all over the fish, inside and out. Arrange the squeezed lemons on the tray and bake for 20–25 minutes, depending on how big your fish is. You will know your fish is ready when the eye has turned white and the dorsal fin comes out easily (the central fin on top of the fish).

Remove the fish from the oven and debone them. Serve the fish, flesh side down, drizzled with the remaining dressing.

Tips: You can use either the whole fish or just the fillets if you are uncomfortable deboning fish – I use the whole fish as the flavour is just incomparable. I also usually get fish small enough so that I can serve one per person rather than one large fish to serve many.

I also love to make this with salmon as the fattiness of the fish is broken down by the tangy, spicy background.

Sumac & Za'atar Sea Bass Tartare

This fresh, light and tangy fish tartare is simple and healthy, but doesn't lack in flavour. Freekeh, za'atar, pomegranate molasses and sumac are now used endlessly around the world, but they have been staple ingredients in Palestine for centuries. It makes me proud that these products are becoming more popular, as they are worthy of being shouted about. These ingredients work so well with raw fish as they elevate it to another level without taking away the flavour of the fish, which should always be the main focus. I am greedy so I would always serve a whole fillet of sea bass per person (between 220–270g (8–9½oz) of meat depending on the size of fish) – trust me, you won't want to share this one.

Serves 2

10 chive sprigs, finely
   chopped

1 spring onion, finely sliced

1 tomato, skinned, deseeded
   and chopped

1 teaspoon sumac

1 teaspoon za'atar
   (see page 17)

1 teaspoon sea salt

3 tablespoons olive oil

1 teaspoon pomegranate
   molasses

juice of ½ a lemon

1 tablespoon green Tabasco

2 sea bass fillets, deboned,
   skinned and cut into fine
   cubes

a small bag of mixed salad
   leaves

Mix all the ingredients, except the salad leaves, together in a large bowl. Taste to check the seasoning and adjust if needed – sometimes the sumac is very sour and za'atar mixtures can vary quite a lot, so you may need more oil or salt to balance the flavours; use your own judgement.

Once you are happy with the flavour, place the salad leaves on the plate, top with a small metal ring mould if you have one and fill it with tartare. Carefully lift off the ring to leave a disc of tartare on top of the salad. Alternatively, just spoon the tartare on top of the salad if you don't have a metal ring. Serve immediately.

Salmon Kubbeh Nayeh
Salmon Tartare with Burghul (Cracked Wheat), Chilli & Garlic

Salmon Kubbeh Nayeh is like a salmon tartare but with a Middle Eastern twist thanks to the herbs and onions it is made with. I like to make little parcels with some onion, fresh mint and a little bit of radish in every bite – it really makes this come alive and it is so clean-tasting. I've eaten this many times but when I ate it at a supper club hosted by the award-winning Middle Eastern chef, Greg Malouf, I realized that I had to include it here; it's such a great dish and also nice to include a salmon recipe as it is often underused in Middle Eastern cooking. I have adapted it slightly by omitting the allspice and changing the quantities as I prefer to have more salmon than burghul (cracked wheat) in my version. There are many different kinds of *kubbeh* in Palestinian cooking. My mother would normally use white fish for this recipe, but the salmon works so well here with the burghul, and the onions, mint and radish all work to cut through the fattiness of the fish.

Serves 4

300g (10½oz) fresh skinless salmon fillet (ask your fishmonger for sushi-grade fish – if you can't find any just make sure it's fresh that day)

80g (3oz) fine burghul (cracked wheat)

1 garlic clove

1 red chilli

6 tablespoons olive oil, plus extra for drizzling

1 teaspoon fine sea salt

1 teaspoon white pepper

2 banana shallots, finely diced

To serve:

2 taboon breads (Middle Eastern flat bread, see page 64)

a bunch of salad radishes

a small bunch of fresh mint

a bunch of spring onions

1 small onion, chopped

Begin by mincing the salmon very finely. You can put this through a mincer, but don't do it more than once, or use a high-speed blender for a few seconds. Take care not to turn this into a thick, stodgy paste. Put it in the fridge until needed.

Put the burghul (cracked wheat) in a bowl, cover with warm water and leave to soak for about 10 minutes. Drain and squeeze any excess water from the burghul. You don't want any liquid in this except for the olive oil.

Crush the garlic and chilli together in a pestle and mortar with 2 tablespoons of the olive oil and mix to a paste. Take the salmon from the fridge and mix it with the burghul, salt, pepper, remaining olive oil, shallots and the chilli and garlic paste. Use your hands to really mix everything together well.

Place the taboon breads on a serving plate and top with the tartare. Make some indents with your finger on the surface of the tartare and drizzle with some olive oil. Serve with all the accompaniments. Tear off bits of bread and make little sandwiches, always making sure you have some onion and mint in each bite as this brings out the best in the dish in my opinion. Simple, clean and delicious.

Bizreh
Za'atar & Lemon Whitebait

I love whitebait and have done so all my life. My mum loved them so much she made us a Palestinian version of them. Once you put one of these delicious bite-sized whitebait in your mouth, you won't be able to stop. They are so simple – just quickly fried and drizzled with fresh lemon juice.

Serves 4–6

100g (3½oz) plain flour
2 teaspoons za'atar
   (see page 17)
2 teaspoons lemon zest
1 teaspoon sea salt
300–500g (10½oz–1lb 2oz)
   whitebait
300ml (½ pint) sunflower oil
1 teaspoon sumac
2 lemons, halved

Put the flour in a bowl and mix in the za'atar, lemon zest and salt. Toss in the whitebait and turn them to coat all over with the seasoned flour.

Put the oil in a deep saucepan and heat to a good hot temperature ready for frying. Fry the whitebait in small batches for about 3–4 minutes – you want them to crisp up and not soak up all the oil and get soggy.

Place the cooked whitebait on kitchen paper and let it soak up all the remaining oil. Continue until all the fish are cooked.

Sprinkle the whitebait with some salt and sumac, squeeze over some lemon juice and serve straight away. Little Middle Eastern fish crisps!

Arak & Dill Grilled Prawns

I ate a dish like this when on holiday in Greece, but made with pasta. The taste of ouzo, which is the Greek version of arak, was incredible. I asked my mother if she had ever had fish with arak before and she told me that she had often cooked us a prawn dish with arak when we were younger, which we loved. The recipe below couldn't be simpler.

Serves 4

150ml (5fl oz) olive oil
4 garlic cloves, sliced
5 tomatoes, chopped
a small bunch of fresh dill
1 teaspoon caster sugar
1 teaspoon sea salt
1 red chilli, deseeded and
   chopped
150ml (5fl oz) arak (or ouzo)
12 large raw Madagascan
   prawns, shell on and
   deveined (see page 193)

Heat the oil in a pan over a medium heat, add the garlic and cook for about 3 minutes to release the flavour without browning.

Add the tomatoes, dill, sugar and salt to the pan and stir together. Add the chilli and mix through. Add the arak and boil to let the alcohol evaporate.

The flavours will have combined sufficiently after about 5 minutes of cooking. Add the prawns and let them simmer until they turn a beautiful burnt orange colour – take care not to cook the prawns too quickly or over too high a heat as this will turn the prawns rubbery. Mix together and serve.

Stuffed Squid with Sweet Potatoes & Coriander

Spiced stuffed squid is a very typical Palestinian dish – it is especially popular in Gaza. The mixture of spicy and tangy ingredients is something I grew up on. In this dish I stuff the squid with an already cooked stuffing mixture so I can just grill them quickly and have a charcoal barbecue effect and flavour. You never want to overcook your squid, ever!

Serves 4–6

4–6 squid

olive oil, for drizzling

chopped red chilli and fresh
    coriander, to garnish

1 lemon, cut into wedges,
    to serve

sea salt and black pepper

For the potato stuffing:

3 tablespoons olive oil, plus
    extra for drizzling

2 sweet potatoes

2 teaspoons sea salt, plus
    extra for seasoning

2 garlic cloves

1 red chilli, chopped

juice of ½ a lemon

a bunch of fresh coriander,
    chopped

2 spring onions, finely
    chopped

Preheat the oven to 200°C fan (220°C/425°F/Gas 7).

First prepare the potato stuffing. Drizzle some olive oil over the potatoes, season with some salt and place them in a baking tray. Add the garlic cloves to the baking tray and bake for about 30 minutes or until the potatoes are cooked and soft all the way through.

Split the potato skins open and scrape out the cooked potato into a bowl. Squeeze the garlic from their skins into the bowl too. Add the chilli, a squeeze of lemon, the coriander, spring onions and salt. Mix in the olive oil and season to taste. Set aside.

Prepare the squid for stuffing. Remove the tentacles from the squid and set them aside. Wash the squid and then pat dry and begin stuffing them with the potato mix. I like to use a piping bag as it makes it easier to inject the stuffing, but you could just use a spoon.

Use a toothpick to re-attach the tentacles while also gently sealing the top of the squid closed to keep the stuffing in place – it doesn't matter if it is not totally sealed, you just want it to be enough so the stuffing doesn't overflow. Repeat for all the squid, place them on a plate and drizzle them with olive oil.

Bring a griddle pan to a really high heat. Place the squid directly onto the griddle to begin searing them – this will char the skin, which adds a delicious flavour to the final dish. Cook for about 3–4 minutes on each side, depending on the size of your squid, until they have turned fully opaque.

Serve the squid straightaway garnished with chilli and coriander and lemon wedges.

Tip: If you are short on time, you can boil the potatoes first, then mash them for the stuffing.

King Prawns with Lemon, Garlic, Chilli & Coriander

My mum always makes this when we have a barbecue, just like her mother did as she was growing up. I recently served this dish at my Jamie Oliver Food Foundation charity dinner and it really was the star of the show. Food doesn't have to be complicated to be divine.

Serves 4

12 raw king prawns (if served as a main, or use 8 for a starter), shell on

3 garlic cloves, crushed

juice of 2 lemons

4 tablespoons olive oil

1 red chilli, finely sliced widthways

a small bunch of fresh coriander, roughly chopped

1 teaspoon sea salt

Use a sharp knife to cut through the skin at the back of the prawns, pushing almost all the way through, but leaving the prawns intact. Open the prawns out to butterfly them and remove their dirt track. Place them in a baking tray.

Mix the garlic with the lemon juice, olive oil and chillies and pour it all over the prawns. Add some of the coriander and mix through. Leave in the fridge for about 30 minutes to marinate.

Bring a griddle pan (or a barbecue grill) to a high heat. Sprinkle the prawns with the salt and gently place them, flesh side down, in the hot pan. Don't move the prawns for 3–4 minutes, as you want them to slightly char but not overcook. You will see the skin start to change colour – once that has happened, turn them over and cook for a minute or so more to make sure they are cooked through.

Remove the prawns from the pan (or grill), sprinkle with a little more coriander and serve immediately.

Pomelo Prawn Salad

This is a light, summery dish that you would find mainly near Gaza, a fishing town where there is an abundance of fish. The trade route through this part of Palestine was very active, so lots of spices, herbs, oils, chillies and citrus fruits were traditionally used in fish dishes.

Serves 2

4 large raw Madagascan prawns, shell on and deveined (see page 193)

a small bunch of fresh flat-leaf parsley, roughly chopped

2 garlic cloves, crushed

juice of 1 lemon

1 red chilli, chopped

2 tablespoons olive oil

a bunch of purslane salad

1 small lambs lettuce

½ pomelo (or grapefruit or orange), peeled and segmented

2 spring onions, sliced lengthways

1 teaspoon sumac

a few edible flowers, to decorate (optional)

For the dressing:

juice of 1 lemon

2 tablespoons white wine vinegar

2 teaspoons sea salt

1 tablespoon caster sugar

1 teaspoon pomegranate molasses

olive oil, to taste

Place the prawns in a shallow bowl. Mix the parsley, garlic, lemon juice, chilli and olive oil in a separate bowl. Pour this over the prawns and leave to marinate for 15 minutes.

Heat a pan over a high heat and once hot, add the prawns, reserving the marinade in the bowl. Cook for about 3 minutes, until the prawns have turned pink and the flesh looks cooked. Set aside to cool slightly.

Break up the purslane and lambs lettuce and mix them together in a serving bowl. Add the fruit of the pomelo and the spring onions.

Mix the dressing ingredients together in a small bowl. Add olive oil to taste and mix the reserved marinade into it. Place the prawns on top of the salad and drizzle with the dressing. Sprinkle the sumac over the top to finish. I like to add edible flowers to make the dish really pop, but this is optional.

Za'atar Clams with Chickpeas, Dandelion & Caramelized Onions

Most of this dish is as my mother makes it. I have added the clams as I think they work well with the meaty chickpeas and add a certain *je ne sais quoi* to the final result. This dish is earthy and cheap – this was the main concern for my grandmothers who were cooking for their eleven and nine children, as they were single parents having both lost their husbands young. Having a big family meant learning to make things on a budget to feed everyone well.

Serves 2–4

500g (1lb 2oz) *hindbeh* (dandelion leaves) – or kale works well if you can't find dandelion leaves

100ml (3½fl oz) sunflower oil

2 large onions, sliced into rings

250g (9oz) clams

1 teaspoon sumac

1 teaspoon paprika

1 x 400g (14oz) tin of chickpeas, drained but reserve the liquid from the tin

1 red chilli, chopped

juice of 1 lemon

2 teaspoons za'atar (see page 17)

sea salt

Wash the dandelion leaves, pat dry and then roughly chop. Blanch the leaves in a saucepan of boiling water for a minute or two and then drain and refresh under cold water.

Heat the oil in a lidded frying pan over a high heat and fry the onions for about 10 minutes until caramelized. Add the blanched leaves and sauté for about 3–4 minutes.

Check and clean the clams, removing any beards and discard any that won't close when tapped.

When the onions and leaves have finished cooking, use a slotted spoon to remove them from the pan and set aside.

Add the sumac and paprika to the pan and toss in the chickpeas with half the liquid from the tin. When the liquid starts to bubble, add the clams and cook, covered with the lid, for a few minutes until the shells have opened (discard any that do not open).

Return the onions and leaves to the pan and add the chilli and a squeeze of lemon juice. Stir through the za'atar, then taste to check the seasoning and add some salt if needed. Serve with bread to mop up the juices or enjoy simply on its own.

Sweet Tooth

No Palestinian home is complete without traditional desserts being on hand at a moment's notice. Our home always had a plentiful selection of sweets and treats, such as walnuts, *ma'amoul* (small shortbread pastries), dates, fresh pistachios and *knafeh* (a sweet cheese pastry) when we were growing up in London. Desserts are a fundamental part of the Palestinian table and are always served with the delicious Palestinian drink, *kahweh bayda* – white coffee – which is hot water, a dash of orange blossom and some sugar, so no actual coffee at all! There are plenty of desserts here that will definitely find a place in your heart. There are old traditional ones and some with a modern twist that my mother and I came up with – whatever you make, I am sure it will satisfy a sweet craving and take you on a delicious and exotic journey.

Yaffa Orange Cheesecake

Yaffa oranges are probably the most recognized oranges in the world. They come from Yaffa, a beautiful town in Palestine where the orange groves are worth writing poetry for. This is where my grandmother Najla originally came from. She absolutely loved it there and had many memories of playing by the sea with her friends and picking oranges, so this recipe is for her.

I don't know what it is about cheesecake that makes it so popular. Everyone has a favourite recipe and their own way of making it. This recipe is foolproof and you can flavour it however you like – I must admit that I like it every way with every kind of flavour because the base is so incredible. In Palestine, my family use a type of cream cheese that we don't have here, but normal cream cheese is fine.

Serves 10

2 eggs

300g (10½oz) golden caster sugar

280ml (9¼fl oz) double cream

700g (1½lb) cream cheese (I use Philadelphia)

1 tablespoon vanilla bean paste

500–700g (1lb 2 oz–1½lb) digestive biscuits, crushed (about 1½ packets)

250g (9oz) salted butter, melted

For the Yaffa oranges:

3 large Yaffa oranges, rinsed and scrubbed

860ml (1½ pints) water

1 clove

1 teaspoon ground allspice

375g (13oz) caster sugar

juice of ½ a lemon

Preheat the oven to 100°C fan (120°C/230°F/Gas ¼–½) and line a 25cm (10 inch) round loose-bottomed cake tin with baking parchment.

Cream the eggs and sugar in a bowl until doubled in volume and very light in colour.

In a separate bowl, start whisking the cream until it has formed a medium to stiff peak. Fold in the cream cheese and vanilla. Add the egg and sugar mix and beat until well combined and thickened.

Mix the crushed biscuits and melted butter together in a bowl and then press the mixture evenly into the base of the cake tin. Top with the cheesecake mixture and level the surface. Bake for 1 hour – the cheesecake will still have a wobble at this point, but it will continue to set in the fridge.

Remove from the oven, leave to cool slightly and then place in the fridge to chill overnight in the tin.

To make the Yaffa oranges, cut the oranges into 5mm (⅛ inch) thick slices and put them in a saucepan with 500ml (18fl oz) of the water. Bring to the boil, add the clove and allspice and continue to boil for 15 minutes. Drain and discard the spices.

Put the sugar and remaining water in a saucepan and increase the heat gradually. Add the orange slices, making sure it doesn't boil, and simmer for 35 minutes. If the water and sugar begin to disappear, add a little more water. The oranges should start to turn transluscent and get sticky.

In the last 10 minutes, add a squeeze of lemon juice and continue simmering. Remove the oranges from the pan and leave them to cool.

After the cheesecake has cooled overnight, top with the candied oranges and serve drizzled with any leftover syrup from the pan.

Awameh
Honey Dumplings

Although this is translated as honey dumplings, there is no honey present; instead, it is a nod towards the sweetness of these gorgeous crunchy dough balls, which are draped and soaked in sweetened sugar syrup. These are traditionally made during Ramadan and are very popular, not only in Palestine, but all over many Muslim countries and in Greece. This is one of those dangerous desserts that you just can't stop eating. I have several recipes for this – one with yogurt, one with baking powder, one with eggs – but I prefer to create this original recipe using yeast, which makes a deliciously crisp dumpling.

Serves 8–10

For the dough:

165g (5¾oz) plain flour
70g (2½oz) cornflour
7g (¼oz) fast-action yeast
200ml (7fl oz) water
1 teaspoon caster sugar
1 teaspoon sea salt
400ml (14fl oz) vegetable oil

For the syrup:

500g (1lb 2oz) caster sugar
300ml (½ pint) water
2 cardamom pods
juice of 1 lemon
a couple of drops of
    lavender oil (this is optional
    and not traditional but I
    use it sometimes)
1 tablespoon *ma'zaher*
    (orange blossom water)

Mix all the dough ingredients together, except the oil, and whisk until you have removed all the lumps. Set aside, covered, in a warm place to rise for about 1 hour.

Meanwhile, begin making the syrup. Bring the sugar and water to a boil in a saucepan and add the cardamom. Once it starts to thicken, after about 5–8 minutes, add the lemon juice and keep reducing for another 3–4 minutes. You don't want it to get too thick though, as it will be soaked in by the dumplings. Add the lavender oil, if using. Remove the pan from the heat, add the orange blossom and stir through. Set aside until needed.

When the dough is ready, put the oil in a large saucepan over a medium-high heat. Test to see if the oil is hot enough by dropping in a small spoonful of batter; if the oil sizzles, it's ready.

Take a teaspoon of batter and roughly shape into a ball, before dropping into the oil. Keep repeating until you have no more room in the pan. Fry the dumplings for about 3–4 minutes or until they turn a golden colour. Once they have hardened and coloured, use a slotted spoon to remove them from the pan and place in a bowl.

Drizzle the syrup over the dumplings and toss them around to make sure they are completely coated. Drain any excess syrup away through a colander, reserving it for another use, and then serve straightaway.

Tip: The dough is easy enough to be handled and shaped into balls. You can add more liquid to make it a runnier batter and then drop spoonfuls straight into the oil, but I prefer slightly shaping mine first.

Halawet Il Jibn
Sticky Sweet Cheese & Cream Wraps

Halawet il Jibn is one of those dishes that we enjoy mainly at celebrations and I often wonder why we don't have it more often as it is so incredibly delicious, yet easy to make. It is a combination of sticky, chewy, melted mozzarella combined with a sugar syrup to make a dough that encases a creamy interior topped with crushed pistachios. These are traditionally made with the delicious, and very famous, akkawi cheese in Palestine and the Middle East, but it is hard to find here, so I often substitute with mozzarella as I have done here. Akkawi cheese is very salty so if you do find it, make sure you cut it and soak it in a bowl of water for about an hour, then drain and soak for another hour before using (or soak overnight). Squeeze it well to remove any excess water. These wraps are also sometimes stuffed with *ishta*, which is a Middle Eastern clotted cream, but you can use mascarpone or ricotta cheese as I have done here.

Makes 24 small parcels

650ml (23fl oz) water
400g (14oz) caster sugar
320g (11¼oz) very fine
   semolina
500g (1lb 2oz) hard
   mozzarella (or akkawi),
   grated
2 tablespoons rose water
2 tablespoons ma'zaher
   (orange blossom water)
40ml (1½fl oz) vegetable oil
800g (1lb 12oz) ricotta
200g (7oz) shelled pistachios,
   crushed

Bring the water and sugar to the boil in a saucepan, then continue boiling for about 5 minutes until it has reduced slightly. Stir in the rose water and orange blossom. Add the semolina and mix continuously. Once it has mixed well, add the mozzarella and keep stirring – don't stop or it will catch on the base of the pan – until the mixture resembles choux pastry and starts pulling away from the edges of the pan. Set aside.

Line 2 thin baking trays with cling film and then drizzle them all over with a very small amount of vegetable oil – just enough to stop the cheese from sticking to the tray.

Tip the dough out onto the trays, scraping the sides to get every last bit. Try and flatten and stretch the dough out so that it reaches all the corners, then leave it to set for about 15 minutes.

Spoon the ricotta into a piping bag and set aside. Take your set cheesey dough and make 2 lengthways cuts and then another 3 widthways cuts to make 12 equal-sized squares in each tray.

Snip a small hole in the end of the piping bag and pipe a little line of ricotta cheese into the middle of each square, then fold the edges into the middle to make a sausage shape. Flip them over so the folded side is facing down, sprinkle with crushed pistachios and serve.

Tip: Usually there would be more syrup drizzled on top, but personally I think the syrup that has been used in the cooking process is enough. If you do want more though, simply follow the first step of boiling sugar and water again and cook until it has reduced by more than half to create a sticky syrup and then drizzle this over the top before sprinkling with pistachios.

M'tabak
Jerusalem's Famous Halloumi & Ricotta Filo Wrap with Lemon Sugar Syrup

This dish is from the heart of Jerusalem. It has been in the Zalatimo family for hundreds of years; they sell this absolutely delicious dish straight from their wood-fired oven to impatient hungry customers. It is a halloumi-based dessert mixed with ricotta cheese, quickly cooked in filo pastry and served with drizzled lemon sugar syrup.

Serves 6–8

500g (1lb 2oz) halloumi

500g (1lb 2oz) ricotta cheese

1 x 270g (9½oz) packet of filo pastry

150g (5½oz) unsalted butter, melted

300ml (½ pint) water

200g (7oz) golden caster sugar

juice and peel of 2 lemons

1 tablespoon *ma'zaher* (orange blossom water)

4 tablespoons crushed pistachios (optional)

Soak the halloumi in a bowl of water for 1 hour to remove any excess salt. Rinse, drain and pat dry and then grate the halloumi into a bowl.

Preheat the oven to 200°C fan (220°C/425°F/Gas 7). Mix the halloumi and ricotta together in a bowl.

Take 2 sheets of filo at a time and cut them into squares, roughly 12 x 12cm (4½ x 4½ inches) in size. Use a pastry brush to brush each square with butter and then layer 2–3 on top of each other. Spoon some of the mixed cheese into the centre and then fold the edges over to seal in any shape you like as long as they are closed – it doesn't have to be perfectly sealed though as it's always good if some of the cheese escapes and bubbles through when cooking.

Place the parcels, sealed side up, on a baking tray. Bake for 15–18 minutes until golden.

Meanwhile, pour the water into a saucepan, add the sugar and bring to the boil. Let it continue to bubble and reduce over a high heat. Add the lemon peel. When the mixture has reduced by half, add the lemon juice and orange blossom water, then take it off the heat and leave it to cool slightly.

When the pastries are out of the oven, pour over the syrup, scatter with pistachios, if using, and serve while the pastries are still hot.

Tip: You can also use akkawi cheese for this recipe, which is more traditional, but can be harder to find.

Ruz Bil Haleeb

Creamy Orange Blossom Rice Pudding with Dried Roses

Rice pudding is a favourite from most people's childhoods. I absolutely adore this dessert. There are always one or two pots lurking in the fridge. It reminds me of family gatherings and happy occasions, as this is when my mother always made it – to celebrate a birth, a party, Eid or a family celebration. The creaminess of the rice and the flavours of the Middle East are so evident in this as the cardamom wafts through with hints of orange blossom, finishing with the crushed pistachios and rose petals.

Serves 6–8

700ml (1¼ pints) full-fat milk

150ml (5fl oz) single cream

90g (3¼oz) cornflour

150g (5½oz) caster sugar

2 cardamom pods, crushed

1 tablespoon vanilla bean paste

150g (5½oz) pudding rice

1½ teaspoons *ma'zaher* (orange blossom water)

20g (¾oz) shelled pistachios, crushed

5g (¼oz) edible dried rose buds

Put the milk, cream, cornflour, sugar, cardamom and vanilla in a saucepan over a medium heat. Whisk the mixture continuously until the sugar has dissolved. Add the rice. Continue whisking and the mix will start to thicken – this should take about 15–18 minutes. If you feel that the mixture is getting too thick and the rice hasn't cooked enough, just add more milk or water. Add the orange blossom water and remove from the heat.

Divide the mix into 4–6 serving glasses, discarding the cardamom pods, and put in the fridge for at least 4 hours to cool and set (although this dish can also be eaten warm if preferred). To serve, sprinkle with the pistachios and some petals from the rose buds. Divine!

Sha'riyeh Bil Sukar

Toasted Vermicelli with Butter & Sugar

When we were young, my mother would make this dish for us all when we were craving something sweet and she was in a rush, as it was so easy to put together.

Serves 4

100g (3½oz) salted butter

5 vermicelli nests, crushed

350ml (12fl oz) water

4 tablespoons caster sugar,
plus extra for sprinkling

Melt the butter in a saucepan over a medium heat. Add the crushed vermicelli and begin to mix and toast until they reach a caramel colour. Add more butter if needed.

Once browned, add the water and 2 tablespoons of the sugar to the pan to soften the vermicelli and cook for 4–6 minutes until the water has evaporated and been soaked up by the vermicelli. Taste a piece of vermicelli to see if it is soft and cooked.

Remove the pan from the heat, add the remaining sugar and mix – the sugar is not supposed to melt, it should be slightly crunchy. Sprinkle with more sugar, if liked, then serve.

Tip: Vermicelli nests often vary in size, so use your judgement and add more or less water or sugar as you see fit.

Sahlab

Sweet Cinnamon Milk

My mother used to make this for us when we were feeling poorly. It is a really simple, sweet and fragrant thickened milk. I love the cinnamon on top as it makes it even more earthy and festive.

Makes 4 cups

750ml (26fl oz) full-fat milk

150g (5½oz) caster sugar

75g (2¾oz) cornflour

2 tablespoons *ma'zaher*
(orange blossom water)

1 tablespoon ground
cinnamon

Put the milk, sugar and cornflour in a large saucepan and heat over a medium heat. The milk should begin to thicken after about 5 minutes, but keep cooking and stirring until it reaches the consistency of double cream or maybe a touch thicker. Keep stirring so it doesn't catch on the bottom and burn and add more liquid if it gets too stodgy.

Once it has thickened, add the orange blossom water and mix. Pour into cups and serve hot sprinkled with cinnamon to finish.

Namoura

Sticky Semolina Dessert with Roses

Namoura are small parcels of heaven. They have all the associations with the Middle East that you can think of – sweet, nutty, sticky, gooey, delicious and fragrant. It is a great dessert to make at Easter if you observe Lent as it doesn't contain any eggs or flour, but doesn't lack flavour. This is a quick and easy dessert with very few ingredients, easy to put together and even easier to eat. This is my Auntie Noha's recipe, which is to die for!

Serves 10–15

500g (1lb 2oz) fine semolina

225g (8oz) golden caster
    sugar

275g (9¾oz) salted butter,
    melted

300g (10½oz) Greek yogurt

1 tablespoon baking powder

edible dried rose buds, to
    garnish (optional)

For the *atter* (sugar syrup):

400g (14oz) golden caster
    sugar

240ml (8¼fl oz) water

juice of 1 lemon

1 tablespoon *ma'zaher*
    (orange blossom water)

Preheat the oven to 200°C fan (220°C/425°F/Gas 7). Line a 23 x 32cm (9 x 13 inch) baking tray with baking parchment.

Put the semolina and sugar in a bowl and mix together. Add the butter, reserving about 20g (¾oz) for brushing. Mix well to make sure the semolina is completely coated in sugar and butter.

Mix the yogurt and baking powder together in a bowl – the mixture will bubble a little. Add this to the semolina and mix well.

Tip the semolina mixture onto the prepared tray and flatten it out – I use the back of a wet spoon to do this. Gently score a diamond pattern on the surface to make it easier to cut once cooked. Brush the surface with the reserved butter. Bake for 35–45 minutes until it has browned on top and a skewer inserted into the centre comes out clean.

Meanwhile, make the *atter* (sugar syrup). Put the sugar and water in a saucepan over a high heat and leave it alone for the first few minutes as you don't want to stir things up and create sugar crystals. Simmer for about 8–12 minutes, until the syrup has coloured slightly and reduced. Once it has reached a syrupy consistency, remove the pan from the heat, add the lemon juice and orange blossom water and stir.

Drizzle the sugar syrup all over the surface of the *namoura* while it is still hot and leave it to soak in for about 30 minutes before cutting into diamonds and eating. Top with rose petals from the dried rose buds, if liked.

Lemon & Rose Doughnuts

These doughnuts are just beautiful. The essence of the Middle East really shines through here with the fragrant rose water, tangy lemon icing drizzled across the surface and the dried rose buds crushed on top. It really has everything I want in a dessert. I know that doughnuts aren't typically Palestinian but they use many of the ingredients found in our desserts.

Makes 18–24

320g (11¼oz) plain flour

250g (9oz) golden caster sugar

1 teaspoon baking powder

1 teaspoon bicarbonate of soda

1 teaspoon sea salt

2 eggs

180g (6¼oz) Greek yogurt

2 tablespoons vanilla bean paste

115g (4oz) melted salted butter (or vegetable oil to make it a chiffon cake texture), plus extra for greasing

1 teaspoon grated lemon zest

For the icing:

250g (9oz) icing sugar

2 tablespoons rose water

2 tablespoons lemon juice

a handful of edible dried rose buds

Preheat the oven to 180°C fan (200°C/400°F/Gas 6).

Mix all the ingredients together in a large bowl to create a smooth batter.

Lightly grease a 6-hole (8cm/3¼ inch) doughnut tin with some melted butter or vegetable oil. Fill the holes in the tin with batter to about one-third full and bake for about 12 minutes until risen and slightly browned.

Remove from the oven and leave to cool while you cook the rest of the doughnuts. It should result in about 18–24 doughnuts depending on how much batter you use.

To make the icing, mix the sugar with the rose water and lemon juice in a bowl until it is a thick white paste.

Dip the doughnuts into the icing or drizzle it over the tops and then immediately scatter the rose petals from the dried rose buds over them so that they stick to the icing.

These doughnuts will keep for 2 days in an airtight container.

Tahini Brownies

These moreish brownies are incredibly sticky, gooey and an absolute necessity in everyone's life! I have made them so many times I have lost count and I can categorically say that I never get sick of them. One piece is most definitely enough – and you can keep the rest to graze on through the week or simply give them to your friends and family. You can also omit the tahini in this recipe if you like but I think that the saltiness just adds something to it – it's not overpowering, just a subtle hint.

Makes 16 pieces

500g (1lb 2oz) dark chocolate (with 70% cocoa solids)

500g (1lb 2oz) salted butter

500g (1lb 2oz) golden caster sugar

160g (5¾oz) plain flour

12 eggs, beaten

8 tablespoons tahini (see page 21)

Preheat the oven to 160°C fan (180°C/350°F/Gas 4). Line a 23 x 32cm (9 x 13 inch) deep baking tray with baking parchment or foil.

Put the chocolate and butter in a baking tray and melt in the oven or in a bowl in the microwave.

Once melted, add the sugar and mix well. Add the flour and mix until no lumps remain. Add the eggs and whisk quickly – this will thicken the mixture.

Pour the brownie mix into the prepared tray and use a palette knife or spoon to level the surface. I gently bash the bottom of my tray on a table to remove any air bubbles.

Start drizzling the tahini all over the brownie mixture and swirl it into the mixture in any pattern you like across the surface. You can of course add more or less to taste – this is really just an addition, not an overpowering flavour.

Bake for about 40 minutes, but check regularly – you want the brownie to still have a slight wobble in the centre. Remove from the oven and leave it to settle and rest for at least 1 hour before cutting and serving.

These brownies will keep for about 4 days stored in an airtight container.

Mandarin Orange Blossom Cake

The simplicity and flavour of this cake will surprise you. It is quick and certainly not fussy, but filled with exotic aromas and a wonderful crumbly texture. The orange blossom and the whole mandarins with skins on leave a slightly floral bitterness that is just delightful. My grandmother and my Auntie Noha used to make something similar to this. They just guessed the measurements and did everything by eye, something not everyone feels confident doing. Baking gives me so much pleasure and I hope it does to you, too.

Serves 8–10

5 seedless mandarins (or 2 large oranges)

150g (5½oz) golden caster sugar

180ml (6½fl oz) olive oil

1 teaspoon *ma'zaher* (orange blossom water)

5 large eggs, at room temperature

320g (11¼oz) fine semolina

4 teaspoons baking powder

a handful of edible dried rose buds, to garnish

For the syrup:

150g (5½oz) golden caster sugar

2 tablespoons freshly squeezed lemon juice

2 teaspoons *ma'zaher* (orange blossom water)

180ml (6½fl oz) water

Begin by scrubbing the mandarins. Once they are washed and clean, place them in a saucepan of boiling water, bring them to the boil, then let them continue to bubble away for about 30 minutes.

Preheat the oven to 180°C fan (200°C/400°F/Gas 6) and line either a 900g (2lb) loaf tin or a 23cm (9 inch) round cake tin with baking parchment.

Drain the mandarins and leave them to cool slightly. Once cooled, blitz them in a food processor or high-speed blender. Transfer to a mixing bowl or the bowl of a stand mixer and add the sugar, olive oil, orange blossom water and eggs. Whisk together until smooth. Add the semolina and baking powder and mix together to a smooth batter.

Pour into the prepared tin and bake for about 45–50 minutes or until a skewer inserted into the centre comes out clean.

Meanwhile, make the syrup. Place all the ingredients in a saucepan over a high heat and simmer for about 6 minutes until it combines and thickens slightly. Set aside until the cake is ready.

When you have removed the cake and it has cooled slightly, prick the surface of the cake with a clean skewer and drizzle the syrup all over the top. It will soak up the syrup and moisten, but the cake is supposed to be a little crumbly and dry with a hint of floral fragrance.

Stud with rose buds to garnish and serve with a hot cup of fresh mint tea (see page 234). The cake will keep for 1–2 days stored in an airtight container.

Tip: Sometimes the baking powder can be very over-active and may inflate the amount of cake batter. If this happens, use two loaf tins to make the cake – if you try to fit it all in one tin, the cake will rise, but then collapse when you take it out of the oven.

Lemon Yogurt Cake with Pistachio Crust

I first made this cake when asked to come up with a sweet cake using yogurt. It was extremely moist with the pistachios giving it an amazing texture that breaks through the wetness of the dough. It is always a great crowd pleaser with a hint of home. This is one of my favourites as it is so moist that it almost feels like it's undercooked, and I love how it's drenched in the syrup making it even more gooey.

Serves 6–8

180g (6¼oz) plain flour

2 teaspoons baking powder

½ teaspoon sea salt

240g (8½oz) Greek yogurt

200g (7oz) caster sugar

3 large eggs

2 teaspoons grated lemon zest

1 teaspoon vanilla extract

120ml (4fl oz) vegetable oil

50g (1¾oz) shelled pistachios, finely chopped

For the syrup:

80ml (3fl oz) lemon juice

150g (5½oz) caster sugar

200ml (7fl oz) water

2 teaspoons *ma'zaher* (orange blossom water)

Preheat the oven to 180°C fan (200°C/400°F/Gas 6) and line a 900g (2lb) loaf tin.

Sift the flour, baking powder and salt together into a bowl.

Mix the yogurt, sugar, eggs, lemon zest and vanilla together in a separate bowl. Slowly whisk this into the flour mixture, add the vegetable oil and then fold everything together gently.

Pour the mixture into the prepared tin and bake for about 45–50 minutes or until a skewer inserted into the centre comes out clean.

Meanwhile, make the syrup. Put the lemon juice, sugar and water in a saucepan and bring to a light simmer until all the sugar dissolves. Remove from the heat, then add the orange blossom water and set aside.

When the cake is ready, leave it to cool for 5–10 minutes, then prick it all over with a few holes and drizzle the syrup over the top. Scatter the pistachios over the top to finish. The cake will keep well for 2–3 days stored in an airtight container.

Banana & Medjool Date Cake

This cake is simply delicious. Gooey, sticky and sweet. I usually eat this warm with a cup of Turkish coffee, sitting in the garden and dreaming of warmer climates. I started making this cake years ago and had great feedback from everyone who tasted it. Use dark chocolate if you like your cake a little less sweet.

Serves 8–10

300g (10½oz) salted butter, softened

300g (10½oz) golden caster sugar

3 eggs

3 bananas, plus 1 sliced for decoration

9–12 Medjool dates, pitted and chopped

100g (3½oz) milk or dark chocolate, broken into pieces

350g (12oz) self-raising flour

1 teaspoon baking powder

Preheat the oven to 160°C fan (180°C/350°F/Gas 4) and line a 27cm (11 inch) round baking tin with baking parchment.

Cream the butter and sugar together until pale and light. Add the eggs and beat again until well combined.

Peel and mash the bananas in a bowl until just smooth with a few chunks. Add to the cake mix with the dates and chocolate and fold in gently, being careful not to overwork. Fold in the flour and baking powder.

Spoon the batter into the prepared tin and arrange the sliced banana on top for decoration. Bake for 60–70 minutes or until a skewer inserted into the centre comes out clean.

Leave it to cool, then serve with tea or coffee. This cake will keep for a day or two in an airtight container.

Freekeh, Fig & Pistachio Cake with Lemon Zest

I love freekeh and use it in so many ways in my cooking. The balance of the savoury freekeh and the figs, with the slightly sweet and salty pistachios really works well. I also add the lemon to give a hint of citrus to bring it all together. My granny would be proud of this recipe – it has Palestine written all over it!

Serves 8–10

285g (10oz) freekeh, ground to a powder in a high-speed blender or spice grinder

2 tablespoons baking powder

1 teaspoon bicarbonate of soda

1 teaspoon sea salt

1 teaspoon ground cinnamon

170g (6oz) golden caster sugar

grated zest of 1 lemon, plus the juice of ½ a lemon

75g (2¾oz) whole pistachios

375g (13oz) Greek yogurt

3 eggs

55g (2oz) melted salted butter

2 tablespoons vanilla bean paste

For the topping:

8 figs, cut in half from root to bottom

50g (1¾oz) pistachios, chopped

a sprinkling of demerara sugar

Preheat the oven to 180°C fan (200°C/400°F/Gas 6) and line a 25cm (10 inch) round baking tin with baking parchment.

Mix the freekeh, baking powder, bicarbonate of soda, salt, cinnamon, sugar, lemon zest and pistachios together.

Mix the yogurt, eggs and melted butter together in a separate bowl. Add this to the dry ingredients, then add the lemon juice and vanilla bean paste. Mix together until well combined.

Spread the cake batter into the prepared tin. Place the cut figs in a circle across the top and scatter with chopped pistachios and demerara sugar. Bake for 30 minutes or until a skewer inserted into the centre comes out clean.

This cake will keep for about 3 days stored in an airtight container.

Tips: If freekeh is a little too intense for you, use 140g (5oz) freekeh with 140g (5oz) plain flour – some people are not used to the intense nutty flavour of it, but I assure you, it is divine.

Don't be tempted to make this cake in a loaf tin – it will not rise properly as the freekeh is so dense. It is always best made in a round cake tin.

Medjool Date Scones

Dates have been harvested by man since before 6,000 BC. There are many varieties of dates but it was the Medjool date that was crowned the fruit of kings. I began making these scones when I became friendly with a girl who was heading up Zaytoun CIC – an amazing community-interest company that is developing a market for artisanal Palestinian produce here in the UK (see page 236). They have the best freekeh, the best za'atar and the best dates – and not forgetting their olive oil – I use them for all of my cooking whenever I can. So I had ordered plenty of dates from them for my restaurant, Baity Kitchen, and used them in everything and thought how perfect they would be baked in scones for breakfast. They worked so well that we had orders for them every day. These scones are delicious and a great way to start the day. Your imagination is the limit as these work well with any flavour. I assure you this is not to be missed if you love baking and love a good meal in one bite.

Makes 16 scones

680g (1lb 7oz) plain flour

1½ teaspoons sea salt

1 tablespoon baking powder

¾ teaspoon bicarbonate
    of soda

100g (3½oz) caster sugar

255g (9oz) very cold salted
    butter, cut into cubes

375ml (13fl oz) buttermilk

200g (7oz) Medjool dates,
    pitted and chopped

1 egg, beaten, for brushing

Preheat the oven to 200°C fan (220°C/425°F/Gas 7).

Put the flour, salt, baking powder and bicarbonate of soda in the bowl of an electric mixer and mix to combine. Add the sugar and butter and mix until it resembles breadcrumbs. Add the buttermilk and chopped dates and mix until you have a nicely combined dough.

Cut the dough into 2 pieces, and then each piece into 8 triangles and place them on a baking sheet. Brush with egg wash, then bake for about 25 minutes, rotating the baking sheet halfway through for an even bake. The scones will keep for 2–3 days if stored in an airtight container.

Tips: If you would prefer a savoury scone, try the Za'atar Scones on page 47.

You can change the filling for this recipe to whatever you like. My favourites are Medjool dates and chocolate, but I often make them with cranberries and white chocolate, tahini and chocolate, or sultanas – the possibilities are endless.

Ka'ak Bil Sim Sim
Sweet Sesame Fennel Biscuits

My family love eating these scented *ka'ak* with fresh mint tea (see page 234), just sitting and chatting together about anything and everything. You will find these everywhere in the Middle East, sold by the bag. They are addictive, crunchy and a little soft on the inside. The lemon zest combines well with the heady aromatic fennel, and the crunch of sesame between your teeth is gorgeous. I adapted this recipe slightly from a blogger called Linda Chabou (La Petite Paniere), who creates wonderful Middle Eastern food. I have tried many recipes but this one is the best – it has everything you would want in a small bite. Heaven!

Makes 15–20 biscuits

500g (1lb 2oz) plain flour, plus extra for flouring

14g (½oz) instant yeast

1 tablespoon baking powder

125g (4½oz) golden caster sugar

2 eggs

100ml (3½fl oz) light olive oil or sunflower oil

grated zest of 1 lemon

1 tablespoon fennel seeds

50ml (2fl oz) warm milk

1 egg yolk, beaten

sesame seeds, for sprinkling

Put the flour, yeast, baking powder and sugar in a bowl if making by hand, or the bowl of a stand mixer fitted with the dough hook, and start to mix.

Add the eggs, one at a time, and continue to mix. Pour in the olive oil and continue to mix. Add the lemon zest and fennel seeds and mix again. Pour in the milk and knead until you obtain a sticky dough. Add some water (about 75ml/2¾fl oz) if needed.

Flour a clean surface, turn out the dough and roll it into a long, thin log about as wide as your little finger. Cut the log into 4cm (1½ inch) slices, roll into a small sausage shape and then join the 2 ends together to form a crown or circular shape. Place them on a floured baking tray, cover and set aside in a warm place to rise for 1 hour.

Preheat the oven to 180°C fan (200°C/400°F/Gas 6).

Brush the crowns with beaten egg and sprinkle with some sesame seeds. Bake for 20–25 minutes or until golden brown. Remove from the oven and leave to cool for 15 minutes.

The biscuits will keep for 1 week stored in an airtight container.

Jallab
Date Molasses & Rose Water

This sweet, intoxicating fresh drink from the Middle East is gorgeously refreshing. I make this during the summer in London and also for special events, but I think it should be drunk more often as it only takes seconds to make and is so good.

Serves 2

4 tablespoons date molasses

2 teaspoons rose water

50g (1¾oz) pine nuts

2 tablespoons golden raisins (optional)

ice cubes

Divide all the ingredients equally between 2 glasses, top up with cold water and mix. Drink on a warm summer's night to refresh you.

Tip: Some Middle Eastern shops sell jallab syrup already made, which you can mix with water, pine nuts and raisins to make this drink, but if you can't find it, then make your own by mixing date molasses and rose water to create the base for this drink.

Ma'zaher Bil Leymoun Wa Shai
Orange Blossom & Lemon Iced Tea

Most of the popular Palestinian drinks are fresh and filled with ice and wonderful aromas. They are made to soothe the harshness of the heat that is endured in the Middle East. I love them even when it's cold outside as I eat and drink to bring back memories more than anything and this drink is no exception.

Serves 2

500ml (18fl oz) water

75g (2¾oz) caster sugar

1 tea bag (I use English breakfast)

juice of 1 lemon

1–2 teaspoons *ma'zaher* (orange blossom water)

ice cubes

nectarine slices and mint sprigs, to serve

Bring the water and sugar to a gentle simmer in a saucepan over a medium-low heat to dissolve the sugar. Add the tea bag, take the pan off the heat and leave it to infuse for about 5 minutes. Add the lemon juice and orange blossom water and mix together.

Serve in tall glasses filled with ice. Add a couple of nectarine slices and a sprig of mint on top and enjoy.

Dibs Rumman Wa Na'Na'
Pomegranate Molasses Drink with Fresh Mint

Palestinians love to use molasses in many dishes and not always just in savoury dishes. Pomegranate molasses have been used in this book for lamb, chicken, desserts and now a drink, making it a real staple ingredient for home cooking. This drink came about just by experimenting and I love it. I have added some extra sweetness to offset the tangy sharpness of the molasses.

Serves 2

500ml (18fl oz) water
150g (5½oz) caster sugar
4 tablespoons pomegranate
  molasses
juice of ½ an orange
a small bunch of fresh mint
ice cubes

Simmer the water and sugar in a saucepan over a medium-low heat until it has dissolved. Add the molasses, orange juice and mint, bruising the leaves gently in your hands to release the flavours before adding, and mix.

Pour into 2 glasses filled with ice and serve.

Kahweh Bayda
White Coffee

White coffee in the Middle East is not coffee as you know it. There is no milk or dairy present, and in fact, no coffee at all! It is simply made using two ingredients and is heavenly.

Serves 2–4

200ml (7fl oz) water
1–2 teaspoons *ma'zaher*
  (orange blossom water)
1 small teaspoon caster
  sugar (optional)

Heat the water in a saucepan until it boils, then take the pan off the heat and stir in the orange blossom water. Stir through the sugar, if using, too. I like to add it for a little more sweetness, but it's entirely optional.

Serve in small Middle Eastern coffee cups and enjoy with any of the desserts in this chapter or simply with a Medjool date.

Kamer Il Deen
Dried Apricot & Pine Nut Nectar

During Ramadan, this drink features at many tables. It is drunk at the beginning of the meal to help lift sugar levels after fasting. It is a beautiful thick, rich, sweet drink that really evokes a sense of home. I especially love the bright orange colour of it. It is made from dried apricot leather, which is extremely well-used in Syria, where most of this product comes from. We used to add sugar to this but nowadays the apricot leather is slightly sweeter than it used to be, so you don't really need any.

Serves 2–4

250g (9oz) apricot leather
480ml (17½fl oz) water
1 teaspoon rose water
ice cubes
pine nuts, to serve

Break the apricot leather into pieces and place it in a bowl with the water. Put it in the fridge and leave it to soak overnight – this will activate the syrup, sweeten it and also make it easier to work with.

Once it has soaked, place the leather and soaking water in a food processor or blender, add the rose water and blitz together.

Serve in ice-filled glasses with pine nuts on top.

Tip: Apricot leather is a solid block of dried and sweetened apricot paste commonly used throughout the Middle East. It is easy to find in most Middle Eastern, Asian and Persian shops.

Shai Wa Na'na'
Fresh Mint Tea

Fresh mint tea is drunk everyday in my house and is very popular all over the Middle East. The mint in this tea is soothing for the stomach and the digestive system so is a great after-dinner drink. It is so, so good for you and absolutely delicious.

Serves 2

450ml (15fl oz) water
2 tea bags (I use any kind of
    black tea)
a small bunch of fresh mint
2 teaspoons caster sugar

Boil the water in a saucepan over a high heat and then add the tea bags and mint. Stir in the sugar and drink it sweet.

Tip: You can also omit the tea bag and just boil water with fresh mint; let it infuse for 5 minutes to really capture the freshness of the mint.

STOCKISTS

UK STOCKISTS
FOR FRUIT AND VEGETABLES:
J Baker of Chiswick
A brilliant fruit and vegetable stall.
Chiswick High Road market stall
Contact: Lee Baker +44 (0) 7956
120128
Email: jbakes@hotmail.co.uk

FOR FISH AND MEAT:
Rex Goldsmith – The Chelsea fishmonger
An amazing fishmonger, who I have been purchasing from for many years.
10 Cale Street, Chelsea, SW3 3QU
Contact: +44 (0) 207 589 9432

Macken Brothers (butchers)
A fantastic butchers where I get all my meat from.
44 Turnham Green Terrace,
Chiswick, W4 1QP
Contact: +44 (0) 208 994 2646

FOR MIDDLE EASTERN INGREDIENTS:
Green Valley
My go-to place for everything Middle Eastern – Halal meat, frozen foods, tinned goods and pulses and grains.
36–37 Upper Berkeley Street,
London, W1H 7PG
Contact: +44 (0) 207 402 7385
Email: info@green-valley.co
www.green-valley.co

Zaytoun CIC
For all Palestinian organic produce.
1 Gough Square, London,
EC4A 3DE
Contact: +44 (0) 207 832 1351
www.zaytoun.org

Sous chef
A great online food and cookware shop with a particularly good Middle Eastern section.
www.souschef.co.uk

Arabica
A great online stockist of Middle Eastern produce.
www.arabicafoodandspice.com

Melbury And Appleton
Online delicatessen with a great Middle Eastern section.
www.melburyandappleton.co.uk

Arez Food
An online Lebanese supermarket.
www.arezfood.co.uk

AUSTRALIAN STOCKISTS
Oasis Bakery
A fantastic Middle Eastern bakery, cafe and online shop.
9/993 North Road, Murrumbeena
VIC 3163
Contact: (02) 61395701122
Email: info@oasisbakery.com.au
www.oasisbakery.com.au

Cedars of Lebanon Groceries
Lebanese and Middle Eastern groceries and Halal products.
Mawson Place, Mawson, Canberra
ACT 2607, Australia
Contact: (02)62902344
www.cedarsoflebanon.com.au

Abu Hussein
Lebanese and Middle Eastern grocery store.
170 Clyde Street, Granville Sydney
NSW, Australia
Contact: (02) 96371261

Baalbek Bakery
Sells fantastic Middle Eastern breads – highly recommended.
99–105 Canterbury Road,
Canterbury, Sydney NSW 2193,
Australia
Contact: (02) 97183870
www.baalbek.com.au

Buy Lebanese
Online shop.
www.buylebanese.com

iGourmet
An online shop with a great Middle Eastern section.
www.igourmet.com

Zaffron Grocery
An online Middle Eastern grocery store.
www.zaffrongrocery.com.au

Abw Foods Australia
An online Middle Eastern grocery store.
www.abwfoods.com.au

PICTURE CREDITS

Page 2: Fiona Dunlop
Page 6, top left: Momen Faiz; top right: Fiona Dunlop; middle: Eyad Jadallah; bottom left: Shareef Sarhan; bottom right: Ahmad Daghlas.
Page 10, top left: Ayman Mohyeldin; top right: Ayman Mohyeldin; middle left: Fiona Dunlop; middle right: Shareef Sarhan; bottom left: Omar Abu Arra; bottom right: Hamde Abu Rahma.
Page 11, top left: Shareef Sarhan; top right: Mohammad Hajj Ahmad; middle left: Omar Abu Arra; middle right: Hamde Abu Rahma; bottom left: Shareef Sarhan; bottom right: Shareef Sarhan.

We would also like to express our thanks to Fired Earth for their kind loan of tiles and to Ceramica Blue for their platters used in photography.

ACKNOWLEDGEMENTS

Before anything, I would like to thank my mother who has always been so patient and understanding, even when I was ruining your life – falling out of windows, getting crushed by horses, jumping from the top of the landing pretending to be Mary Poppins and cracking my jaw – I mean this list can go on and on. This is how I knew you would be supportive of me and all my choices because you were always there for me. I became a chef because of you. Thank you for going through the book with me to make sure I was doing justice to your family and their recipes. Thank you Mama for being you and for loving me.

To my dad, who is a huge influence in my life. I would like to thank you for always pushing me to be the best I can be, especially with my choice to be a chef as it just made me want it more. It took some time for you to understand my passion but I always knew that you were proud. Now with this book to document our history and food from your home, I hope you can see my passion for us as Palestinians. You made us all love Palestine and want to be a positive image of it – I hope you are proud. I love you.

Heather Holden Brown, thank you for believing in my book and for constantly being supportive. We made a fabulous book!

Jacqui Small, thank you for seeing past a title and really embracing my history and beautiful culture. Thank you for letting me keep it as true to our past, and capturing memories from my family to pass down to generations. Thank you for creating such a beautiful book.

Fritha Saunders, thank you for really giving me a voice. It really shows that my family and I had a lot of involvement creating this beautiful book.

Thank you Manisha Patel for all your hard work and thought that went into every millimetre of every picture. Those long days were totally worth it in the end.

Ria Osbourne, literally every picture is beautifully shot and shows the true essence of what the dishes were like when my grandmother made them. Thank you!

Lucy Harvey, your styling ideas and prop options were spot on every single time. You really got into the theme of Palestine and all its colours and beauty. Thank you.

Abi Waters, thank you for your patience and support throughout this process. Who knew how difficult it was getting this all done, but you made it seem so easy.

To all my friends and sisters, nephews and nieces who listened to me go on about the book, asking questions day after day, trying the food and being part of every moment of making this book. I love you all.

Thanks to all my aunties and grandmothers, who made this book come alive – with all the memories that we have, we could write volumes. Thank you for being so colourful and descriptive in the stories and recipes that you have shared with me. I love you all. This is a tribute to you all.

To Nadia, I love you. You are my 4th sister.

Thank you to Mariam and Suma, who were always there to help out and get dishes ready with me for the book. You really made the journey easier for me. Thank you!

Thank you to Rex Goldsmith for supplying me with the best fish I have ever eaten in all the years of knowing you.

Thank you to J Baker for supplying me with wonderful fruit and vegetables and our lovely chats in Chiswick.

Thank you to the Macken Brothers for always providing me with top-notch meat and the best service ever.

Steph, thank you for pushing me to start this Palestine On A Plate project. Look how it blossomed!

And finally to everyone who has been through this up and down journey of mine over the last few years. Thank you for being there and always being supportive of Palestine and my food and the hard work that goes into putting a positive light on my country. Thank you to you who have bought the book, I hope you enjoy it as much as I have enjoyed writing it and capturing my past. It has truly been an honour doing this and very emotional.

X Joudie

INDEX

Joudie Kalla has been working as a chef in London for 16 years. She is of Palestinian descent and focuses her cooking around this particular Middle Eastern cuisine, all the while removing misconceptions of Middle Eastern food being little more than greasy kebabs by creating healthy, vibrant, moreish dishes that are easy to make and packed full of goodness reminiscent of home. She trained at the prestigious Leith's School of Food and Wine and has worked at restaurants such as Pengelley's (a Gordon Ramsay restaurant), under Ian Pengelley, Daphne's and Papillon with chef David Duverger who allowed her to flourish and follow her dreams of focussing solely on this style of cooking from her heritage.

Joudie has been running her own private catering company for over seven years and ran a hugely popular Middle Eastern deli and restaurant, Baity Kitchen, for three years in Chelsea (it closed in February 2013). As well as accepting private commissions, Joudie holds regular supper clubs. She has cooked for Loyd Grossman (who was also a regular at the deli) when he has hosted fundraising dinners for the Royal Drawing School, and also hosted Palestinian-themed dinners for the Mosaic Rooms and Jamie Oliver's Food Foundation.